THE MAD ONES

CRAZY JOE GALLO
AND THE REVOLUTION
AT THE EDGE OF THE
UNDERWORLD

TOM FOLSOM

WEINSTEIN
BOOKS

To the Revolution

"The only people for me are the mad ones, the ones who are mad to live, mad to talk, mad to be saved, desirous of everything at the same time, the ones who never yawn or say a commonplace thing, but burn, burn, burn."

—JACK KEROUAC

Author's Note

New York City is cleaner and safer now than it was when Crazy Joe Gallo got gunned down in front of Umberto's Clam House on Mulberry Street in the early hours of April 7, 1972.

Joey's world was cigarette-fogged nightclubs on the East Side. Gangland killings in the barbershops of ritzy hotels. Dingy pads in jazz-fueled Greenwich Village. He dressed in spit-shined Italian loafers and skinny black ties. He rode in a 1955 Cadillac and ran the jukebox racket. He and his brothers holed up with shotguns in a dilapidated tenement on the crooked South Brooklyn waterfront and waged guerrilla war on the desolate streets of Red Hook.

The tale of the Gallo brothers has been recounted in the lore and legend of New York City, including Bob Dylan's ballad, Jimmy Breslin's comic novel, and fictionalizations in *The Godfather* trilogy, but I felt that no non-fiction book captured the madness of the Gallos. I had to recreate his world to understand why he did what he did. I read what Joey read and studied his heroes—the strangers in Camus, the outsiders in Sartre. I pieced together a case dragged out from half a century ago. I interviewed those who had been on the scene firsthand. I waded through almost 1,500 pages of unpublished FBI files on Joey Gallo and culled what made sense from the least reputable sources: Wiretaps of underworld conversations. Leads from informants.

In order to reconstruct the narrative in a fast-paced, as you are there immediacy, I was forced to choose between multiple and contradictory versions of past events, some that could only be verified by the victims. Three books I kept within reach included one of the best cop books to come out of the mean streets of New York City, *Chief*, by Albert Seedman, Inspector Raymond Martin's *Revolt in the Mafia*, and Donald Goddard's *Joey*, filled with interviews from the women left behind in the wake of Crazy Joe's murder.

None of the dialogue has been made up.

Names have been changed to protect the innocent and preserve the reputations of the dead.

King of the Streets

The body rested comfortably in tufted velvet eggshell, dressed in a double-breasted navy blue pinstripe suit with a dark blue shirt and deeper blue polka-dot tie. A bouquet lay below the folded hands, right over left, the right ring finger decked out in a large square blue stone. A gold cross and chain hung around the neck. A lithograph of Jesus hung on the bright pink curtain behind the bier.

Carmella knelt beside the bronze coffin at the private family viewing in the baroque Morgan Room, paneled in dark wood with ornamental wallpaper. Dim chandeliers hung from the high ceiling. Among the wreaths of red roses, orchids, and yellow and white chrysanthemums, a book made of flowers lay open on a stand, spelling out in petals, "To My Brother, Joey Gallo."

For nearly an hour in the funereal quiet, Carmella stroked her brother's slicked-back hair and kissed the mole on his cold cheek. Joey could've taken the Gallos to greatness in a dynasty to match the Kennedys. The papers wrote only the bad things about him, but Carmella knew the possibilities, cut short by a hail of bullets at Umberto's Clam House in the heart of Little Italy.

"Blood in the streets!" screamed Carmella. "The streets are going to run red with blood, Joey!"

Joey's mother, Mary, fainted. She wore old-country black. Four young men carried her downstairs to the basement parlor of Guido's Funeral Home, a Greek Revival brick mansion built by robber barons. Someone held smelling salts under her nose.

"My Joey, my Joey, what did they do to my Joey? What did they do to my Joey?"

The night before, a doctor had been sent to Mary's wood-frame, asbestos-shingled rooming house in a rundown section of Flatbush to administer tranquilizers. He walked in and saw a bunch of guys standing around. He was told not to say much.

"What happened to her son?" asked the doctor.

"He had an accident," said one of the guys.

Mary's portly and bald seventy-one-year-old husband now sat on a chair in the corner of the funeral parlor.

"He's all right," remarked an onlooker. "Don't worry. He's been ready."

According to an FBI informant, Umberto, the bootlegging father of the three notorious Gallo brothers, "raised his sons to be hoodlums and killers," "encouraged them in their criminal activities," and influenced them to "remove all competition in their illegal enterprises." His eldest, Larry, was buried with a thick purple ring around his neck, seared into his flesh by a manila cord. The baby of the family, Kid Blast, was the last living son. Handsome, with thick muttonchops down his cheeks, Blast dutifully attended to his grief-stricken mother. Mary cursed at a woman whispering consolation in her ear and renounced the heavens, shouting, "Jesus Christ? Jesus *Christ?* You know I don't believe in Jesus Christ!"

On this clear blue Sunday in South Brooklyn on April 9, 1972, two hundred mourners filed into the Morgan Room to say goodbye to Joey.

Jacques Levy, the shaggy-haired director of the madcap off-Broadway play *Scuba Duba*, stood before the bier. Years later, during a late night with Bob Dylan, Levy would recount this sad day when sitting down to write "Joey," an eleven-minute ballad on the flip side of the Hurricane Carter story on Dylan's album *Desire*.

"I never considered him a gangster," said Dylan of Joey. "I always thought of him as some kind of hero in some kind of way. An underdog fighting against the elements." Dylan crowned his eponymous hero "King of the Streets," nobler than the fool in *The Gang That Couldn't Shoot Straight*, the gangster farce by hard-boiled newspaperman Jimmy Breslin. Inspired by the Gallo gang, the novel featured a band of ragtag crooks led by Kid Sally Palumbo, played in the film version by the city's favorite lanky actor, star of stage and screen, side-burned Jerry Orbach.

Orbach made his name over a decade before playing El Gallo, the bandit star of the hit musical *The Fantasticks*. Looking down on his dead friend, he couldn't help but regret playing Joey as such a bumbling idiot in *The Gang That Couldn't Shoot Straight*.

"Breslin's book had portrayed Joey as a clown," Orbach told *Time* magazine. "Then when I met Joey, I was absolutely amazed to find out that maybe he had been a wild kind of nut before he went to prison, but something had happened to him inside."

"Joey had an intense sense of destiny," added Jerry's wife, Marta. "If he was truly marked for dying, this old-fashioned way—in style—would have been a point of honor to him. He was afraid he would choke on a piece of steak or slip in the bathroom."

Marta and Joey forged a friendship over hours in the kitchen of her Chelsea brownstone. She towered over him as he sipped his coffee spiked with anisette. Joey affectionately nicknamed her the Big Job. "I loved Joey. I've said that from the moment I met him. He was like a member of my family," Marta told *Women's Wear Daily*, the foremost authority on the newest rage in New York City. Radical chic was out. Gangster chic was in.

"He almost became one of the Beautiful People," dapper author Gay Talese told *WWD*. "I went to a dinner party about a month ago in the home of Linda Janklow and all they did was talk about Gallo."

High society had more to chew on after Joey's murder, which sent "a shudder throughout the social and literary circles of New York," reported *WWD*. Susan Sontag, the skunk-haired voice of the city intelligentsia, regretted her missed opportunity. "I wish I'd had the chance to talk to Joe Gallo before he died," she said.

Ironically, Jimmy Breslin was to be the keynote speaker for the upcoming A. J. Liebling Counter-Convention—a gathering of journalists who revolutionized reporting in a fiction-inspired style known as New Journalism. Joey was supposed to be the mystery guest. The convention's chairwoman, Nora Ephron, was "not to tell a soul," she later revealed to the *Washington Post*, "because they might come here and shoot him."

Joey had been slated to join writer Gore Vidal, radical Abbie Hoffman, film director Otto Preminger, and political powerhouse Bella Abzug to discuss the topic "How They Cover Me." His death made for page one news. Paparazzi staked out spots to pop off the bereaved coming in and out of Guido's Funeral Home. Tough guys threatened a *New York Post* photographer, leaving Pete Hamill, already a tabloid veteran in his mid-thirties, to paint the scene in his column.

"The first time I saw Joe Gallo," wrote Hamill, "he was standing against the far wall of the Ace Pool Room on Church Ave. in Brooklyn. He was wearing a wide-brimmed pearl gray gingerella hat, a dark blue shirt with a white tie. A few of the Irish guys laughed when they saw him; he looked too much like Richard Widmark in *Kiss of Death* to be true, but then someone suggested that we shouldn't really laugh. The guy's name was Joe the Blond and he was packing a gun."

Joey was a little guy, listed by the NYPD as 5 feet 6 inches. Small, like the toughest guys in the B-pictures, Jimmy Cagney or George Raft, the steely henchman in the original gangster epic, *Scarface*. In his teens, ruling the corner of Fourth Avenue and Sackett Street as King of the Cockroach Gang, Joey flipped a silver dollar, Raft's signature move. Joey wasn't going to be stealing copper piping from Brooklyn brownstones for the rest of his life. He was going to make it to the big town. Give big lunks the score.

"I could have worked my way up to head soda jerk at Whelan's Drugstore," said Joey, "but what kind of life is that for a guy like me?"

In 1949, nineteen-year-old Joey sat in a South Brooklyn movie theater, likely smoking in the back row. The lights dimmed and the silver screen faded in to the evening skyline of New York City. PARK CENTRAL HOTEL blinked down on the urban jungle.

In the Tombs, the city jail, psycho killer Tommy Udo sneered at a cop walking past his cell.

> UDO
> For a nickel I'd grab him. Stick both
> thumbs right in his eyes. Hang on till
> he drops *dead*.

Tough guys weren't supposed to be blond, blue-eyed, and wiry, but pretty-boy radio actor Richard Widmark stole the film noir classic *Kiss of Death* in his breakthrough role as the unhinged Tommy Udo. Decked out in a black suit, black shirt, and white tie, Udo set out at night for Club 66. A juicy dame at his side, he sipped Château Martin at his usual table and snapped his fingers to the fast beat of the jazz combo, riffing, "How da ya like that music, man? Right upstairs. Send it, Jack!" Then he got to work.

"You know what I do with squealers?" asked Udo, right before he ripped out the electrical cord, tied the old hag to her wheelchair, and dumped her down the rickety steps. "Let 'em have it in the belly, so they can roll around for a long time thinking it over."

In the dingy bathroom of the Gallo home in Flatbush, blue-eyed Joey stood in front of the mirror and pulled a comb like a switchblade. At four, he'd taken his father's straight razor, sliced off his golden locks, and shook them in a fist at his pale blonde mother, who'd cursed him with sissy curls. Now, slicked back with a goop of Wildroot Hair Dressing, the hair made him a dead ringer for Tommy Udo. He called himself Joe the Blond.

"You got two ways to go," figured the Blond. "You need money or nerve. You wanna new suit? You don't have the money? Steal one. Looks just the same. Feels even better, if you don't get caught."

The Blond boosted a crate of twenty men's suits from the warehouse. He put on a black double-breasted jacket over a sleek black shirt. He knotted his white silk tie and hit the streets. His Udo grin was unnerving, something like the Joker in the *Batman* comics. Joey's high-pitched giggle filled dead spots with menace. He got off on making guys squirm. "Laugh at Joe the Blond," concluded Pete Hamill, "you're liable to get your brains blown out."

Hamill gave the city its first in-depth look at the Blond in the summer of 1961, in a *New York Post* profile titled "Brooklyn's Joe Gallo—Young Hoodlum of the Old School." Joey made for the best tabloid copy since the bad days of Prohibition, when Al Capone would pose for shots on his way to the opera house, angering President Hoover and sparking a drive to "Get Capone!" After that, mobsters longed for obscurity, preferring to run things without any heat from the press, but Joey stood outside of the courtroom and wisecracked to the television cameras.

"How can I be afraid when my bodyguard is with me?" he once told NBC man Gabe Pressman. The camera panned down to Mondo the Midget, official mascot of the Gallo gang. The pugnacious dwarf scrunched up his face. Notorious for impromptu press conferences, Joey loved getting his name in ink, and kept his clippings in his back pocket to show around to his gang. He phoned reporters when they forgot to print his infamous nickname, Crazy Joe.

Immortalized in black and white in a *Life* magazine cover story, "Death Throes of the Gallo Mob," Joey and his brothers posed for the cameras, looking like gangsters were supposed to look in cheap black suits and skinny black ties. "He should've been in show business," said Albert Seedman, chief of detectives of the NYPD.

Instead, Joey played out his wildest film noir fantasies in the Naked City, dressed like Cagney, right up until the bitter end.

"Joey always looked good in blue, except that now you could not see the tormented eyes," wrote Hamill about the body lying in state in the Morgan Room. "They seemed to range from the color of slush to the color of fogged blue steel. They watched everything . . . For a few years, in the early '60s, I would see him in police stations, along with his brothers and some of the other hard guys from South Brooklyn; he would joke with the cops, and smile for the reporters, but the eyes never changed."

Sitting in a parked blue Cadillac across from Guido's Funeral Home, plainclothes detectives from NYPD Intelligence drank stake-out coffee. Nobody knew who killed Crazy Joe, but it was no secret that he had it coming. "More than anyone else," predicted a cop years before, "this guy reminds me of Legs Diamond. Legs was crazy too, and wouldn't play ball with any of the other racket guys. Eventually he got shot down. That's what'll happen to Joe Gallo too."

Early Monday morning, cops combed through the mob scene gathered outside of Guido's. Most in the crowd were rubberneckers, waiting hours to see a real live gangster, even if he was dead. It was something to tell the grandkids, that they'd seen a guy who inspired *The Godfather*, which had been earning a million a day at the box office since it opened a month before. Fans wondered if Kid Blast would "go to the mattresses" to revenge his family, like Sonny Corleone did after his brother Michael wasted that Turk in the old-time spaghetti joint.

Shortly before ten, NYPD blue coats parted the crowd to make room for the main attraction. Cameras snapped Joey's widow, Sina, walking out of Guido's into the cold morning light. Dark Jackie O's hid her puffy eyes. She looked lovely so sad, her lush dark hair parted down the middle. Sina, the Gallo family dream girl. She kept Joey well fed and, as a dental assistant, ensured that his teeth were perfectly maintained. After three weeks of marriage, she watched her new husband get gunned down at Umberto's Clam House after a second serving of scungilli salad.

"I want to kiss my Joey," cried Mary. "They took away my Joey and I want to kiss my Joey."

Five of the guys had to help Mary down the steps of the funeral home. They shouted at the paparazzi and placed her in the limousine at the head of the procession. Tucked away in the rear, twelve limos back, sat the darkly gorgeous ex-wife, Jeffie, sole survivor of a doomed love, played out over steamy Village nights filled with starry beatnik dreams. Death was the only way out for Joey.

"When he knew he was in a corner and couldn't beat it," said Jeffie, "then he said, 'Fuck it. I'll die. I'll die before I say I'm sorry.' Life or death, it always had to be his way."

Eight jowly pallbearers slipped the coffin out of the side door, bearing the weight of a thousand pounds of gleaming metal between thick shoulders and fleshy necks. The waxed black hearse turned onto Clinton Street, a strip of renovated brownstones with sandstone stoops and religious yard shrines, and made its way toward the western edge of South Brooklyn. It crossed the noxious Brooklyn Queens Expressway, the BQE, clogged with six lanes of blaring horns and angry Monday morning commuters, and entered Red Hook.

⚊⚊⚋⚋⚊⚊

"In the old days, this block was moving," claimed the guy at Mastellone Brothers, a *salumeria* a block over on Union Street. Two doors down used to be Z. Giama's Italian-American Grocery, between the Boston Fish Store and the Jersey Pork Store. In a black shirt and a white apron, Giama would greet customers who came on pilgrimages from all over Brooklyn via the crosstown trolley line to buy imported provolone and cans of tomato paste, stacked in a pyramid in the storefront window.

Families pushed baby carriages along the sidewalks of Columbia Street to get their portraits taken at Virgilio's Photo Studio. Kids sipped malts made with Borden's Ice Cream at Ben's Luncheonette. V. Scalia had hats for sale. La Tosca Music Shop sold radios. Alexander Clothiers peddled off-the-rack zoot suits.

Bustling with frantic gestures and sidewalk haggling, Columbia Street was the heart of Brooklyn's Little Italy until the New York City highway czar, Robert Moses, declared it a slum. Hell-bent on connecting his Brooklyn Battery Tunnel to the Brooklyn Bridge, claiming it was necessary to evacuate and defend the borough in case of war, Moses wrote off the locals as insignificants in his master plan. "What can you do?" said the candy-store owner. "These were mostly immigrants here who were afraid they might get deported if they protested. You can't fight City Hall."

In August 1946, Mayor O'Dwyer broke the ground with a

chromium-plated pick, paving the way for the earthmovers to dig mile after mile of trenches. From the penthouse floor of the nearby Marguerite Hotel, Robert Moses watched his obsession unfold. "And I'll tell you," said one of his men. "I never saw RM look happier than he did when he was looking down out of that window."

Instead of paving his expressway along the western water-front to build a stunning esplanade on top, as he did for the more well-to-do neighborhood of nearby Brooklyn Heights, Moses cut off Columbia Street from the rest of the borough and let it die.

The funeral procession made its way down the tiny sliver of neighborhood at the edge of the Red Hook waterfront. The baby carriages were gone. There were boarded-up stores and rubble-strewn lots. Cops from the 76th Precinct waiting at the corner smelled the morning whiffs of the Gowanus, the stinking canal that bubbled alongside the oily Buttermilk Chan-nel, and directed the hearse onto President Street.

Grandmothers peeked out from behind frayed and yellow-ing lace curtains hung in the windows of rundown tene-ments. Elderly men stood at the curb and took off their hats as a sign of respect to a last breath of life on the block. Few had forgotten that summer day a decade before when Joey showed up with none other than Huntz Hall. To the Mod Squad, Joey's nickname for the bell-bottomed hippies in the Gallo gang, Huntz stood two spots to the left from Dylan on the cover of *Sgt. Pepper's Lonely Hearts Club Band*. To the old folks, Huntz was Dippy, one of the Dead End Kids, a pack of street urchins who ran amok in Hollywood's golden years, starring in juvenile delinquent hits like *You're Not So Tough*.

"It was like the Pope showing up at the Mardi Gras hand

in hand with a clown," remembered an outsider, stunned to witness the regal treatment Joey received on President Street. "They loved him. He was their protector. You could see it in their faces. 'Ah, he's a *good* boy. I don't care *what* he does—he looks after us.'"

In the summer, a kid could earn a dollar for opening the door of Joey's Cadillac. Swarms of boys begged for nickels to get lemon ice. Men stood up from their domino games in respect. Little old ladies hobbled down the steps to pinch the big mole on Joey's cheek. He doled out cash like a drunken uncle and didn't write names down in a black book. To an old crone refusing a fifty, Joey snapped, "Hey, I'm going to get angry, Grandma!"

The hearse passed a newly built swimming pool with a gazebo, built by the Gallo gang for the neighborhood kids. It stood out against the rest of the grime on this last block of President Street, which ended at the waterfront. Across the street sat the Longshore Rest Room, the brownish pool hall and luncheonette run by Mondo the Midget. In brighter days, sunlight streamed through its plate-glass front window, decorated with a Kent Cigarettes ad. Black fedoras hung from wooden pegs as the gang dealt rounds of pinochle at the linoleum diner tables and cracked open frosted bottles of Piers from the metal cooler.

Here reigned Punchy, Tarzan, Louie Cadillac, Peanuts, Bull-eye, Mooney, Bullshit, Vinnie the Sicilian, Roy Roy, the Worm, Big Lollypop, Little Lollypop, and a rogue's gallery of hoods slipping in and out of the Gallo gang, averaging twenty-five strong over fifteen years. Like Lady Liberty, who looked over the Red Hook waterfront, the Gallos embraced the wretched refuse of the South Brooklyn underworld, hoods who didn't stand a chance in the Italian-only Mafia—Sammy and Louie the Syrians, who were a pair of silent tough guys from the Arab strip of Atlantic Avenue, along with Egyptian knife-thrower Ali Baba.

Sitting in the limo, thick, curly-haired Pete the Greek, Joey's bodyguard, winced at the pain in his backside. That bullet, from the same batch of lead that lodged into Joey's spine, would keep the Greek from dancing the *sirtaki* for a while, which he gracefully performed to the shouts of "Oppa! Oppa!"

Looming to the right of the procession was the old Gallo headquarters, 51 President Street, a weathered three-story brick tenement. Joey used to keep Cleo the lion in the basement, a score he got through an exotic animal dealer. To collect on an overdue loan-sharking debt, Joey would bring the deadbeat to the cellar door and throw down a piece of raw meat. Cleo roared.

The now-abandoned storefront used to be the site of the Direct Vending Machine Company, distributors of pre-mix soda across South Brooklyn, brainchild of the late Larry Gallo. Here at 51 President, armed to the teeth with a stockpile of shotguns, the brothers decided to expand their enterprise in a bloody and hopeless revolution against the Mafia.

"They may take my sons," swore Umberto, "but a lot of them will go too."

Joey's hearse stopped outside an abandoned church at the end of President Street, where decades before, worshippers flocked for evening vespers, invigorated by the fresh air off the waterfront and the sight of barges chugging down the

Gowanus Canal. In 1941, a last Mass was held upon the news
that Moses would destroy the neighborhood with his BQE,
parting Red Hook like the Red Sea. Marching up President
Street toward their new church on Carroll Street, the faithful held aloft their saints in a grand procession and left behind
the damned.

Umberto stepped past the rusted iron gates into this long-
abandoned church. For fifteen minutes, as the dusty half-dome
windows shrouded the light, mourners prayed for his son's soul.
Some of the guys went across the street to the JCJ Social Club,
next to Gargiulo's Florists, the old funeral home with its huge
clock ticking down time. In a week, after the dirt settled on
Joey's grave, fifteen mattresses would be delivered to the JCJ
basement.

The procession entered the gothic gates of historic Green-
Wood Cemetery, winding its way through paths draped in
budding cherry blossoms. Wingtips flattened the grass toward
the open grave dug in the side of a grassy knoll. A green
tent blocked the ceremonies from the FBI surveillance
cameras, filming through the one-way window of a panel
truck. Rose after rose dropped onto the coffin as the
priest, imported from Cleveland, read the Rites of Christian
Burial.

"My baby, my son," wept Mary. Her tears fell down the ancient well of sorrow, where mothers tasted the wounds of
fallen sons so that vengeance stained the tongue. She hurled
herself onto the coffin, crying, "Take him with you. Take Big

Boy." Dark lenses shielded the eyes that looked to the last hope for the family, Kid Blast. "Get that Big Boy, Joey." Big Boy. The tall hit man who took down her Joey. "Take him with ya, Joey." Two gravediggers lowered Joey next to his brother Larry, united in death as they had been in life.

"You really wanna know what my problems are?" Joey once asked. "Time and place. That's all. If I'd have been born at the right time and the right place, they'd have put my statue up in the streets." Instead, it was a flat stone on the ground in Lot 40314.

The procession drove down the hill. Umberto sat lost in memory.

In 1920, he bade farewell to his home on the coral seas of Torre del Greco on the shore of Naples and stowed away aboard the SS *Canapich* of the White Star Line bound for Boston. He dreamed of fortune to come. He could carve beautiful images out of shells and stone. Surely they had an eye for beauty in America. Years later, he was living in a cold-water tenement at 47 President Street, making a paltry living engraving for Diagonale & Sons on Fulton Street. On the night of the deal, he stood at the edge of a wood-slatted pier, drenched by the torrent of rain, and saw the faint outline of the approaching boat, stocked with Scotch in a dry era. The boat was within meters when gale-force winds began pushing it back, returning it to darkness . . .

Umberto told the limo driver to stop. He held up the procession for five minutes as the limo turned around and returned to the gravesite. Kid Blast continued onto President Street.

"If that boat had landed," said Blast, "my father could have been another Joe Kennedy, and who knows what might have happened to us boys then?" Maybe he would've sailed with Jack, Bobby, and Teddy at Hyannisport, instead of swimming with Larry and Joey in the Gowanus Canal, filthier than the Ganges.

Hollywood B-Grade

"Was the blood coming out of your ears also by this time?" asked Bobby Kennedy.

"I couldn't open my mouth at all," testified Sidney Saul in February 1959, before the morning session of the U.S. Senate Select Committee on Improper Activities in the Labor or Management Field, the McClellan Committee. "My jaws felt as though they were locked at the end, and I could barely talk. I went to the mirror to fix myself, and fixed my shirt, and my face, and washed my face, and my nose was completely out of shape, and it was formed like a horseshoe, like a U, and as a matter of fact, it is out of shape now because of that."

The trouble began two summers before, the season that brought in a hit single from Buddy Holly. Sidney got a morning service call from Wagon Wheels, a luncheonette on his route that housed one of his twenty-two jukeboxes. The repairman phoned in the damage report. He told Sidney that the front glass of the juke was smashed in. The guy who did it got on the line. He wanted to see Sidney in person.

"Well, I don't know who you are," said Sidney. "I certainly am not going to come down and see you."

The guy said he was the brother of the owner, and if Sidney didn't come down now, he'd smash the machine to bits and see that it was thrown onto the street. Sidney made an appointment to see him that evening. Ernest waited at the curb. In Sing Sing they called him Kippy. He wanted to take Sidney someplace so he could talk to somebody. Sidney hated leaving his car unattended. It was dark out.

"If you don't want to leave your car here," said Kippy, "I will go in your car and tell you where to go."

Sidney passed Caccio's Meat Market along Fourteenth Avenue at the edge of Bensonhurst. Kippy asked how Sidney got his jukebox in Wagon Wheels. Sidney got it fair and square. He purchased the location from the owner more than two years ago. They had a contract.

Sidney kept straight, but Kippy's conversation went off the regular path. He started threatening.

"Threatening you *how*?" asked Senator McClellan, the chairman.

"That he would kill me," said Sidney. "And they would find my body lying off the Belt Parkway."

"What did he want? What was he wanting?"

"He didn't make sense in his conversation as to what he actually wanted. I was trying to read between the lines and pacify him."

Kippy repeated his threat like a scratched B side, at least five or six more times. Then he said to take a right. Sidney parked in front of Jackie's Charcolette, a greasy-spoon diner, named after Joey's sister Jacqueline. Downstairs from the Ace Pool

Room, locals knew it as a family restaurant. Guys in sharkskin suits regularly jumped behind the grill to help the cook, stocky, light-blonde Mary Gallo, flip fifteen-cent burgers. Jackie's had a reputation. Columnist Jack Lait had pictures snapped from across the street for his scandal rag, *Confidential*, a sordid look at the New York City underbelly.

Mary's eldest now sat inside drinking coffee and smoking cigarettes. His high-buffed Italian wingtips shone like freshly minted nickels.

Joey was the flash of the Gallo brothers, but Larry was the boss. "A genius. He could take your watch apart," admitted Detective Charlie Bartels. Larry had a head for opportunity and was always on the prowl for which South Brooklyn joints could use a jukebox, the crown jewel of the Gallo family business. The eldest, it was his duty to ensure the Gallos were given their due.

A polite young man and an immaculate dresser, Larry told Sidney to sit down, have a cup of joe. Sidney was jittery enough. Larry asked how many machines Sidney had on his route.

"Eight," lied Sidney.

Larry said he had eight machines too. He suggested they partner up. Sidney could run the route. Larry would have nothing to do with it. Sidney could operate the business himself. Larry told Sidney he'd be well off if he went in with him.

"I told Mr. Gallo that I had a very bad taste about the business," testified Sidney. "I didn't care for it, and was anxious to get out of it. I had been in it more or less to pay off some debts because of a previous business loss, and that I was trying to straighten myself out . . . I believe Mr. Gallo thought I was sincere about what I said."

Larry had a baby moon face to trust. He wrote his number

on the back of a business card from Local 26, the Cafeteria
Workers Union. Sidney took it out of courtesy.

"What was Kip doing during this period of time?" asked
Kennedy.

"During the conversation a few times Kip started threatening me again, and finally Mr. Gallo sent him out."

"Again, that he was going to kill you?"

"Well, he said—he didn't actually say that he would kill me
in the restaurant, but he said they would find my body off the
Belt Parkway, which was practically the same thing."

Kippy was much friendlier when Sidney ran into him six
months later. He wanted Sidney to sign up for Local 19, the
new jukebox union. Sidney heard rumors about that union, a
problem union run by "bad boys." Sidney couldn't be of any
value. He only had one jukebox left, he said, the one at Wagon
Wheels.

Kippy said it didn't matter, that it would help him a great
deal if Sidney went back to Jackie's and saw Mr. Gallo, who had
all of the forms that Sidney needed to sign. Sidney said he'd
go over and sign at his convenience.

Two months later, in the midst of a hot meal with his family, the telephone rang. The guy on the line asked if this was the
Sidney who had the jukebox at Wagon Wheels. He wanted to
see him right away. Sidney couldn't do that. He was having his
dinner.

"Unless I see you at Wagon Wheels very shortly, your machine will be out in the gutter."

Sidney arranged an appointment for eight o'clock that
evening.

"I called my service telephone number," testified Sidney,
"and told the operator that I was going in to meet somebody

that I did not know and didn't like the sound of it, and if everything was all right I would call her back within a half hour, and if I didn't call her back within a half hour for her to notify the local police that something was wrong."

That night Wagon Wheels was packed with regulars. The owner's wife flipped burgers behind the open grill. Sidney was directed past the soda fountain, up two steps, to Charlie and Dutch's table in the rear. Dutch was fresh out of Sing Sing on murder. Charlie had a long rap sheet, including disorderly conduct with dice. He stared across the ketchup. Nobody said much of anything for the next twenty-five minutes.

Sidney excused himself. He called his operator on the pay phone in the parking lot and told her there didn't seem to be anything wrong. The fellows just wanted to ask him a few questions. She should forget the instructions he gave earlier. Two or three minutes after sitting back at the table, Sidney got smacked across the jaw with an open palm.

Charlie asked what Sidney was going to do for him. Charlie wanted to partner up. Sidney didn't want to partner with Charlie. He wanted to get out of this business completely. Charlie wanted five hundred dollars.

"I didn't know you knew these fellows," said Kippy, coming out of nowhere to join the table.

"I just met them," said Sidney.

"You never signed up with nineteen, did you?"

Dutch put a nickel in the jukebox. He wasn't choosy. He only needed it loud. He returned to the table and pushed away his seat. Kippy took off his short jacket and draped it over the back of his chair.

"I started pleading with them," testified Sidney, "and it didn't seem to have any effect."

"This fellow is an actor," said Charlie and Dutch.

Charlie held a chrome napkin holder above his head and threatened to bash in Sidney's skull if he said anything else. Kippy kept punching.

"If you haven't got five hundred dollars," said Dutch, "give them three hundred dollars. It is cheaper than buying a new set of teeth."

Sidney bled heavily from his right nostril. His mouth felt like it was full of sand. He began to slump. Charlie ordered a coffee for Sidney and had it brought to the table, in plain sight of everybody.

Diners looked right through Sidney. The owner's wife kept on behind the counter. Sidney wasn't even finished with his coffee when Kippy was back at him. He beat heavier this time, much heavier than before, making Sidney bleed from the ears.

Sidney felt himself slide over to his subconscious mind. He could hear Charlie tell Kippy to stop. Kippy didn't stop. He punched away like a wild man until finally Charlie shouted, "*Lascialo!*"

Kippy retrieved his jacket and walked out. Charlie ordered some more coffee and straightened Sidney's tie. Sidney couldn't chew food for three weeks. Sidney broke down at the awful memory. His sobs echoed off the marble walls of the packed Senate Caucus Room. Reporters leaned against the columns and scribbled notes. The chairman paused to let the horror sink in.

"Call the next witness."

"Mr. Lawrence and Mr. Joseph Gallo."

Larry and Joey walked up the red carpet in a slow two-step shuffle, dapper in black suits. A skinny black tie dropped from Larry's white collar. Joey's jet-black shirt was buttoned to the top. He wore big black sunglasses. Pretending not to notice the flashguns popping on the other side of the table, the brothers waited for their cue.

"Do you and each of you solemnly swear the evidence you shall give before this Senate Select Committee shall be the truth, the whole truth, and nothing but the truth, so help you God?"

They did. Both sat down and lit smokes.

"Mr. Joseph Gallo," began Kennedy, "could you tell us where you were born, just a little bit about your background before we get into the union business?"

Joey mugged a three-quarter profile for the Channel 5 camera, showing off the big mole on his cheek. The arc light warmed his smooth, angular face. He leaned toward the mike.

"I respectfully decline to answer because I honestly believe my answer might tend to incriminate me."

A three-tiered crystal chandelier sparkled above. The joint was decked out better than the Copa. Joey sunk back into the leather-studded chair.

"Just a little bit about your background," asked Kennedy. "Where you went to school. Can you tell us that? Where did you go to school?"

Joey's arm jerked in a sudden, spastic motion, sending two glasses of water and an ashtray sailing off the table, soiling the red carpet with wet ash and cigarette butts. "I respectfully decline to answer because I honestly believe my answer might tend to incriminate me."

"Mr. Joseph Gallo, how did you happen to go into the union business, in Local Nineteen? Did you feel that the workingman was having a difficult time? That you could help and assist him?"

"I respectfully decline to answer because I honestly believe my answer might tend to incriminate me."

Bobby laid the Harvard sarcasm on a little thicker. "What was it in your background and record that made you want to go into the union business, to try and help and assist your fellow workingman?"

"I respectfully decline to answer because I honestly believe my answer might tend to incriminate me."

Bobby turned to Larry. "What about you, Mr. Gallo? What made you decide to go into the union business?"

Larry opened his cupid bow lips, more Botticelli than the poster boy of the Rackets Committee. Joey put a hand on his older brother's shoulder and whispered in his ear. The room waited anxiously.

"I respectfully decline to answer because I honestly believe my answer might tend to incriminate me."

The chairman deepened his scowl line. In his two years chairing the Select Committee, Senator McClellan had seen a range of witnesses, from pipe-wielding enforcers to the brass ring, Teamster boss Jimmy Hoffa. Usually he let Kennedy play bulldog, but these two rascals deserved nothing short of an old-fashioned Arkansas-style whuppin'. The chairman pointed his bony finger like a hickory switch.

"Do you know Sidney Saul? You, Joseph?"

"I respectfully decline to answer because I honestly believe my answer might tend to incriminate me."

"Larry, how 'bout you?"

"I respectfully decline to answer because . . ."

"Do you know anybody in this country that you could admit you know without self-incrimination? You, Mr. Larry?"

"I respectfully decline to answer . . ."

"Do you have a wife?"

"I respectfully decline to . . ."

"Are your father and mother living?"

"I respectfully . . ."

"Are you an American citizen?"

"I respectfully decline . . ."

The chairman took a smoke from the pack. These boys drove him to it. "How about you, brother Joseph? Are you a racketeer and a gangster? Are you what is known as a thug or a hoodlum? Is that the classification or category you would come in?"

"I respectfully decline to answer because I honestly believe my answer might tend to incriminate me."

Kennedy dug into his trick bag as the McClellan Committee's chief interrogator. He needed to engage Joey as he did Hoffa, whom he took on in five-minute staring contests. Hoffa winked to throw him off. Kennedy pegged him a little girl under a layer of smell, a mix of sickly sweet perfume and fat-man sweat. The bully didn't even have the guts to do the dirty work himself. Hoffa bragged about his underworld muscle, saying any union boss who didn't use it was a fool.

Teamster Local 266 employed the best in the business, the Gallo brothers. The FBI had close to nothing on the boys. Hoover was more worried about Communists than the underworld. Kennedy knew better.

On November 14, 1957, New York State troopers caught sixty-five of the top criminals on the eastern seaboard, gathered for a clandestine gangster convention in an eighteen-room stone mansion on a remote hilltop in upstate Apalachin. It was proof enough of the existence of the Commission, a shadowy nationwide Mafia crime syndicate with an all-powerful reach that rivaled the Vatican or the Rothschilds. An enemy within, the greatest threat on American soil.

"If we do not on a national scale attack organized criminals with weapons and techniques as effective as their own," swore Kennedy, "they will destroy us."

In attendance at the Apalachin meeting was the Olive Oil King, Joe Profaci, picked up with one of Larry's business cards in his wallet.

———⚜———

Bobby rolled up his sleeves and loosened his tie. Backing him up on muscle were forty overworked staffers in the basement of the Old Senate Office Building, which was packed with coffee cups, mounds of paperwork, and, as his brother Jack put it, vig-ah.

Like the men who beat poor Sidney Saul, Bobby had a flair for the shakedown. He made B No. 250889, aka Joe the Blond, sweat it out in the reception room before the big show. Gangsters hated keeping early-morning hours, but this spry hood just jumped up at a guy who walked into the office and riffled through his pockets, and said, "No one is going to see Mr. Kennedy with a gun on him. If Kennedy gets killed now everybody will say I did it. And I am not going to take that rap." Swaggering into Bobby's office, he ignored the Churchill quote on the wall—*We shall not flag or fail . . . we shall never surrender*—and knelt down to feel the rug. "Nice carpet ya got here, kid. Be good for a crap game."

If they weren't bulbous like Hoffa, reasoned Bobby, they were lean and cold and hard like this one. Blond curls grazed the back of the kook's neck in a ducktail. The files connected him with the murder of a Brooklyn tavern owner and unwanted competitor in the jukebox racket, shot so many times in the face they couldn't identify him except from dental records. Bobby asked about the victim.

Joey giggled.

Bobby couldn't help but notice his twitch, like a Tourette's case. He was smaller than expected. He took another look at this Gallo fellow, who had just offered one of his secretaries a job, promising she could take as much as she could steal from the till. Gallo wasn't insane, as the file reported. It was a pathetic act from an attention-seeking shit. Bobby couldn't wait to tear him apart at the big show.

At the Senate Caucus Room, Bobby stared through his horned rims, across the witness table and into Joey's black shades, which blocked a good read on his eyes. If Jack were here, as he should've been as a standing member of the McClellan Committee, they'd have had a field day. But Jack was off running for president, leaving Bobby to give this Hollywood B-grade gangster his best shot in front of the television cameras.

"You would have somebody like Mr. Saul knocked off, but you wouldn't do it yourself, would you, Mr. Gallo? You would have somebody go and do it for you, wouldn't you? Do you find it is much easier to have a big man go and do it? Rather than a little fellow like you?"

Joey lolled his head around the room. "I respectfully decline to answer because I honestly believe my answer might tend to incriminate me."

The chairman worked himself up like the preachers in the backwoods of his home state. A huff of smoke trailed from his nose and mouth. Witnesses trembled on the rare occasions he unleashed the Wrath of Heaven, as they called it on the committee.

"Are you a physical coward?"

"I respectfully decline to answer—"

"That might incriminate you to answer? Do you think it would? Do you think it would—"

"I respectfully decline to answer because I honestly believe my answer might tend to incriminate me."

Wrath became an exasperated sigh.

"Senators," asked the chairman, "have you any questions for these talkative witnesses?"

Jowly old Sam Ervin, country lawyer from the Blue Ridge Mountains in the heart of North Carolina, raised his massive brow and asked in all dumbfounded sincerity, "Can yew boys tell us of an honest day's work you ever did in yo' life?"

Larry took the mike. "I respectfully decline to answer because I honestly believe my answer might, you know, tend to incriminate us."

Dismissing the brothers, Chairman McClellan called John Amalfitano to the stand. Having had his fill of hoodlums for the morning, he wasted no time getting to the point.

"From the information we have, you are just a plain, sorry gangster. A parasite upon humanity. Do you wish to make a comment on that?"

"Point of order, Mr. Chairman," Kennedy stated for the record. "I would like to say that this witness is not in the same category, according to our investigation certainly, as the Gallo brothers. The Gallo brothers are in a far lower category, and far worse than this man that appears before the committee."

At the end of the morning session, the Gallo entourage met at the bottom of the marble steps of the Caucus Room.

"You damn labor racketeer, you gangster," ribbed Joey, smacking Amalfitano's thick head with a rolled-up newspaper. "Aren't you ashamed of yourself?"

The pack roared. Joey left the gang to go chat up Kennedy's assistant.

"Mr. Kennedy is a better fellow than I thought he was," said Joey. "We really appreciate him saying that nice thing about Amalfitano. It shows he is very fair." If there was anything he needed, a few bucks, or someone taken care of, Joey said to call on him.

Bobby rushed down the steps, off to nail more gangsters in the time he had left. He found his calling as chief counsel of the McClellan Committee, but soon he'd have to give up the work he loved to run the campaign for Jack, groomed to take the family to the White House. Joey cornered him on the way out and promised, "I'll line up my people for your brother in 1960." He called over five or six of the boys and made each pledge a vote for JFK.

"The second biggest favor you could do me is to keep your preference quiet," said Bobby, "and the biggest favor would be to announce for my brother's opponent."

Joey howled at his long-lost twin, separated at birth by a night of stormy weather.

Crazy Joe

All of his life they told him he was nuts. Dropping out of the Brooklyn High School of Automotive Trades to work at Louis Auto Repair, sixteen-year-old Joey got a severe case of the jitters after being in a bad car wreck. There was no evidence of a nervous disorder, but the hospital diagnosed him as "unable to work because of his extreme restlessness." Months later, Joseph Gallo enlisted in the Navy but refused to answer the questions necessary for his induction. He was honorably discharged in 1946 after the Great Lakes Naval Hospital found him "temperamentally unsuited for further military service manifested by restlessness and a nervous disposition."

On April 6, 1950, Joe the Blond turned twenty-one inside the psych ward of Kings County Hospital. He was sent here for observation after he showed up at the courtroom in a zoot suit, ready to beat the rap on possession of burglary tools. The magistrate found him "incapable of understanding the charges against him." The shrinks declared him "presently insane."

In 1959, Joey got his infamous nickname. He claimed it came after he showed Kennedy up on national television by looking so good in his suit, an event recounted in RFK's 1960 bestseller, *The Enemy Within*.

"I read that bullshit," spat Joey, taking a *New York Post* reporter between the lines. "And just for openers I didn't have a black shirt on. I was wearing a one-buck work shirt I picked up at an Army-Navy store on Sixth Avenue.

"I walk into Kennedy's office and he's got his sleeves up and his tie down and he says, 'So you're Joe Gallo the jukebox king?' The first thing he told me was if I helped him get Hoffa, I'd never want for nothing. When I told him the hell with that and that I was going to take the Fifth, he said, 'You're not so tough—I'd like to fight you myself.' And when he came around from behind his desk and started to peel off his coat, I told him, 'I don't fight,' and I reached in my pocket and pulled out a mezuzah that Sid Slater had given me and shoved it in his face."

No way was Joey going to play rat on account of big league politics.

"Plenty of people have said to me, 'You know, Joey, if you'd gone another way, you might have made something of yourself. If you'd put your brains and your energy into something legitimate, you could have gotten to be President.' And you know what I always say to them? 'Bullshit. I couldn't be that crooked.'"

Weeks after Joey came home from Washington, the cops picked him up on the charge of vagrancy with no visible means of support.

"They say I been picked up fifteen, seventeen times,"

complained Joey. "That's junk. I been picked up maybe a hundred and fifty times and they never make a record. I get picked up for vagrancy and for consorting with known criminals—my father and my brother, in my own house."

The judge sent the Blond back to the Kings County psych ward, hoping to keep him off the streets for a while. The shrink administered the Rorschach test.

"It looks like somebody spilled ink on it and folded it over," said Joey.

The shrink probed the Blond's creative impulse, telling him to draw a house, asking, "Would you like to live in a house like this?" Next, a tree. "Is this tree alive? How old is it?"

Joey put aside his artwork and laid it straight. "If I could answer questions like that, I would be crazy."

"I spoke to this psychiatrist," Joey told the *Post*, "and I said to him, 'You're appointed by the police commissioner, aren't you?' And he said he was. And I said, 'Look, I been accused of a lot of vicious crimes. It happens I know a lot of people who met violent ends and that's my crime. And now they're trying to railroad me and you tell me I've got a persecution complex. And I told him I have a large family and a lot of friends and if I was him, I wouldn't let myself be used as a tool of the commissioner and the DA and be the one to drop the axe on me."

Joey brought up his older brother, Larry.

"He never lifted a hand to nobody in his whole life. He's a mechanic, and the government says he's Public Enemy Number One or Two. I forgot which because I'm the other one."

The shrink noted "dysocial reaction," less severe than

Joey's previous diagnosis of "dementia praecox, paranoid," the archaic term for paranoid schizophrenia.

A free man, Joey slipped into his Caddy and shot like a bullet across the Brooklyn Bridge, cruising the steely skyscraper canyons like a shark. Yellow cabs and sleek limos passed as he turned onto East Fifty-second Street. A valet opened the door. Joey greased the palm. He flicked his lighter and sucked deep. He turned his homburg over to the hatcheck girl, who waved him upstairs to the gilded bar. Under the chandeliers, bartenders shook expertly mixed concoctions—martinis, gimlets. The headwaiter ushered Joey to his usual table in the spacious art-nouveau dining room.

This sparkling new nightclub, the Arpeggio, was raved about in the "Goings On About Town" column in *The New Yorker*. The high priestess of society, Joan Crawford, showed up in white mink and arched eyebrows to hear the club's mainstay, Bobby Short. Torching his famed "Tabasco piano," Short burned up the ivories as he threw back his head and sang Cole Porter until the early hours of the morning. Slumming on Park Avenue. Breezy jaunts to Rio. Haiti. All for the taking.

Candelabras flickered as the top Italian chef on the East Side circuit cooked up the specialties. Diners were bathed in soft light against flowing drapery. Oscar, the house pianist, played the interlude. Husbands told their secretaries not to stare, but there he was, the tough guy who stared back at them over their morning coffee, front and center in the *New York Herald Tribune*, the day after he faced off against that dashing Bobby Kennedy. His suit fit perfectly, black with white pearl buttons.

On another evening, complete with a white silk tie, Joey sat at the table of an East Side nightclub with his "date" Cleo, purring on a leather leash. Patrons asked why nobody called the cops on the wild cat.

"Because that guy is Crazy Joe Gallo," said the headwaiter. "I'd rather wrassle the lion than mess with Crazy Joe."

The Barbershop Quintet

Shortly before midnight, a pregnant teenager, her name withheld here to protect her reputation, stood waiting on the dimly lit corner of East Thirteenth Street and Avenue P in a quiet section in South Brooklyn. Her husband wouldn't take her back. The father was long gone. Due in two months, her last hope was Frank Boccanfusco. She had met him two months before, when he was fresh out of Green Haven State Prison on a burglary bid. He had promised to marry her and had signed his name on the proper prenatal records. Later, he realized this arrangement jeopardized his parole. Frank was not the father of the child, but "the methods used by him to have his name removed from the records has annoyed members of both families," read the police report later filed on this hot August night in 1959.

The girl tracked down Frank at his hangout, a luncheonette nearby on Eighty-sixth Street in Bensonhurst, and asked him to come and meet her on the corner. Frank agreed, but knowing the reputation of the girl's family, brought two friends to the rendezvous. Leaning into the open window of their

Ford sedan, the girl asked Frank if they could take a walk, just the two of them. Frank peered down the block and saw three guys lurking about. True to his suspicions, the girl had set him up.

Frank told his friend to step on it. A jet black Buick waiting in the shadows kicked into gear and cut them off. A blue and white Olds screeched in from the rear at the other end of Thirteenth Street. It was quiet enough to hear the crickets as the four doors of the Buick opened. Four guys got out, one with a moon face and an Italian Beretta. Larry stuck it through the window and pointed it at Frank's head. Another ordered everyone out of the car. A third hung back with a Luger. The situation turned worse when Joey ran out from behind a tree with a thick tow chain wrapped around his hand. He whipped Frank while the girl watched. Frank's friends got hit with tire irons.

Softened up for the ride, Frank and friends got stuffed into the backseat of the Olds. Larry sat in the middle of the long leather front seat, crouching around to face Frank with a pointed gun, intermittently taking it by the barrel to pistol-whip some sense into him. Joey sat beside Larry with the chain. The Olds sped a block down toward Quentin Road, where Frank's cries were less likely to wake up the neighbors. Frank got out, hands on his head, but when a red Italian sports car slowed to watch the commotion, he ran to it, screaming for help. Larry grabbed the crowbar and got a last whack in before Frank hobbled into the sports car and sped off to safety.

Larry straightened himself up. Always neat as a pin, Larry hated to look out of order. He picked up the poor girl, who had fallen out of the Olds onto the street, sprawled out and crying in hysterics.

The eldest of the Gallo brothers, older than Joey by two years and Kid Blast by three, it was Larry's responsibility to right all wrongs to his family. The trio of brothers might nearly come to blows with each other in the midst of screaming chaos, but there was no question of loyalty. Once at 4:15 in the morning on October 23, 1954, on the second floor of the American Legion Hall by Jackie's Charcolette, a plain-clothes cop restrained Kid Blast so that his fellow officers could arrest him. He didn't have a warrant. Joey decked him in the face.

Two years before, in 1952, Larry took one for Joey, who was in the early stages of his Udo phase. The two brothers had been using the family phone in Flatbush to help run the local Italian lottery. The Rackets Squad busted in, searched the closet, and found a crate of twenty men's suits that Joey stole from the warehouse.

Mary fessed up, swearing that a man on the street had sold it to her. Larry swore that a man on the street sold it to *him*. He took the rap for Joey and got a year in the Tombs on stolen goods.

Larry did good time and got bumped up in the ranks of the $2.4 million policy operation of racket kingpin Frankie Shots, boss of the numbers game in Bensonhurst. Pleasant-looking, with a face sagging from age, Shots ran the lottery. Everybody loved Frankie Shots. He had kids, including his own son, Tony, run numbers at the diners and malt shops. Waitresses and clerks plucked lucky numbers from thin air, hoping their one in nine-hundred-and-ninety-nine combination would match the last three digits of the track-bet tally in the *Daily News*.

As the rising star of Shots' operation, Larry earned a spot

on the waterfront, where he was guaranteed action from the longshoremen.

Everyone who worked the docks was to play numbers whether they liked it or not, on orders of the big boss, Tough Tony, who got kickbacks on all underworld activity on the waterfront. Tough Tony had plenty of schemes to squeeze money out of the longshoremen—like the mandatory haircuts at a union-backed barbershop, paid for in advance, cuts the barber never even gave.

Italian longshoreman Pete Panto decided he'd had enough. Tired of having to borrow money from the loan sharks scouring the piers so that he could afford to pay kickbacks to the hiring bosses, Panto rallied a thousand men to the cause and shouted, "We are strong! All we have to do is stand up and fight!" A week later, on July 14, 1939, Pete Panto disappeared. Scrawled across the piers, the question emerged in Italian: *Dove Pete Panto?* Where was Pete Panto? In Jersey, rotting in a lime grave under a chicken yard across the street from Dirty Face Jimmy's brother-in-law's place. He'd been strangled in a waterfront shack on the orders of Tough Tony's brother, Albert Anastasia, the Lord High Executioner of Murder, Inc. Exclusive to the Commission, this organized hit squad from South Brooklyn wiped out scores of troublemakers who threatened the underworld order. In return for the corporate efficiency, the Anastasia brothers got to rule the docks.

Dove Pete Panto?

The graffiti lingered on the piers when Larry worked the waterfront. Reminders of duty to family were all around. His father taught him the only way to the top in South Brooklyn. It wasn't carving beauty out of stone.

The Gallos had big rewards in store if they did dirty work for the mob. As the eldest, it was Larry's responsibility to steer the Gallo ship. His father had taken the first leg, leaving behind the azure shores of Torre del Greco for the oily Buttermilk Channel in Red Hook. Larry planned to take the family from the stinking Gowanus to the shores of the Great South Bay in Long Island. The good life.

Larry impressed Frankie Shots, talent scout for the Syndicate, but Shots didn't make it to the big leagues by taking numbers from longshoremen, or get to run a $2.4 million policy bank by being nice to the neighborhood grannies who placed their bets under the beauty parlor hairdryers. They didn't call him Shots for nothing.

⚞⚟

On the morning of October 25, 1957, Albert Anastasia leaned on the ticket booth of the Park Sheraton Hotel, advertised as a "Hallmark of Hospitality" in the heart of Manhattan's theater district. Tourists were lining up to see *West Side Story* in its second smash month at the Winter Garden. "Ugly as the city jungles," raved the *New York Times*, "and also pathetic, tender and forgiving." Society types raved about it on opening night. The bloodthirsty, revenge-fueled gangs roaming the streets of Hell's Kitchen a few blocks south were now seen as misunderstood lost boys, searching for meaning the only way they knew how. Anastasia could've gotten good seats if he gave a damn about gangs of ballet dancers. The almost two grand of cash in his pocket carried a lot of clout at the Park Sheraton.

"Very much the gentleman, nice to deal with, a man with a real love for kids," remembered Douglas du Lac, the hotel toy-store proprietor, offering the kindest statements on record about the hated and feared Anastasia, the Butcher of Brooklyn.

Anastasia stepped away from the booth at about 10:15AM and walked into the hotel barbershop.

"Haircut."

Joe the barber got Chair #4 ready. Anastasia unbuttoned his white shirt and took a seat. The glass mirror reflected the flat nose. A wicked receding hairline left more hair on his gorilla chest. He was known as the Mad Hatter because of his taste for hats. Proud of the last of his locks, nice and thick in the back, Anastasia got a trim twice a month at the Sheraton. Joe wrapped the hot cloth around his beefy neck. Anastasia closed his eyes and eased into the chrome chair. The shaver ran up the back of his neck and toward the left side of his cheek. Fluorescents hummed under the clipper buzz. Bullets hit. Anastasia kicked off the footrest. He jumped to his feet but they shot him in the back. He crashed into the glass shelving. A bullet dropped into his underpants.

"Death took the Executioner," began Meyer Berger's cover story in the *New York Times*. Cropped for public decency, the crime scene photo looked like a Weegee. A beefy arm stretched out from under the piles of white towels. A patch of sunlight hit the tiled floor, a mix of blood, hair, and bay rum aftershave.

There were no positive IDs on the killers, who hid their faces behind bandanas, fedoras, and dark-green sunglasses, but the guy at the flower shop fingered a group of four or five men heading for the Fifty-fifth Street exit.

The big shave was the talk of the town at the glitzy supper clubs along Manhattan's gangster-ridden East Side nightery belt—the Red Carpet, the Tender Trap, Chi-Chi, the Living Room. Every gangster needed a nightclub on which to hang his fedora.

Most nights, twenty-eight-year-old Joey Gallo double-parked his 1955 black and green Cadillac on East Fifty-second Street outside of the Harwyn Club, a pink-and-black Stork Club knockoff, then made his way over to the Club Playboy on East Fifty-sixth Street and Lexington Avenue (not to be confused with the Playboy Club, with its bunny-eared and cotton-tailed cocktail waitresses).

"Just whistle, and Playboy will roll out the red carpet!!" read the advertising postcard, featuring a top hat, cane and gloves, and a martini. Cocktails and hot hors d'oeuvres began at 4 PM. The house pianist, Harry "Ain't Misbehavin'" Brooks, played his famous tune night after night as patrons enjoyed the softly lit, intimate atmosphere, "a new innovation in Supper Club Dining," with its superb delicatessen kitchen featuring hot corned beef, pastrami, and salami, as well as steaks, chops, and lobster.

Before the State Liquor Authority closed the joint down, Joey's B-girls perched on stools until four in the morning, chatting up suckers for $2.50 champagne cocktails, which the bartender mixed with cheap Rhine wine and a soda spritz. The scam was knocked back with a pink-lipstick smile. The jukebox showcased the latest hits. On Friday night, a week after the Anastasia hit at the Park Sheraton, it was "Jailhouse Rock" by Elvis.

Joey called over three of the girls to keep the boys company. He waved over his manager, the pudgy, bald Sid Slater, and bragged, "From now on, Sidney, you can just call the five of us the Barbershop Quintet!"

"I just kept sipping my drink, hoping that the girls were too dumb to catch on," remembered Sid. "It's even possible that Joey was boasting, having his kind of a joke. He always did have a funny sense of humor. But I believed him then, and I still do."

Pizzu

The Gallos pushed jukeboxes in Frankie & Johnnie's, the Lovelle Bar, Red's Pizzeria, Cardiello's Bar & Grill, and the Holiday Arms. Kids plunked milk money into the sleek, shiny chrome beauties, flashing pink and electric green at a dime. Metal arms dropped forty-fives, spinning them like a whirling dervish. Critics claimed the jungle beats hit the bloodstream like a dope fix, whipping the after-school bobby-sox set into a sex frenzy, turning the malt shop into a cradle for juvenile terrors. Frank Sinatra scorned "the martial music of every sideburned delinquent on the face of the earth." In South Brooklyn soda shops, teens in ducktails held their turf at the counter, sitting on the stools with hobnail boots against the opposite wall, so no one could pass. T-shirts bulged with rolled up Luckies yanked from the cigarette machines, another Gallo venture. Soon the Gallos branched out into blinking pinball machines, feared as the gateway to hard gambling.

In time, the Profaci Family, the ruling class of South Brooklyn for over three decades, took up the issue of whether the Gallos should be "made" men. A few capos didn't think they were the right kind of people. Too reckless. Joey was weird and had to be on the *babania*, they said, the junk. A compromise was reached. Larry would be accepted, but before the capos gave the oath to Joey, a guard would have to watch him in a hotel room for two days, to see whether he'd break out in withdrawal sweats.

Joey was livid about having to take the mob drug test, but Larry twisted his arm.

"How can it hurt? The tab will be on them."

It was everything Larry had hoped for since Frankie Shots scooped him up to run numbers. Two brothers in the Profaci Family. Larry liked the sound of that. Joey owed him one for the stolen suits. After two days of free room service, Joey swore the Mafia oath of silence. They didn't burn a picture of the family saint like they used to, but the sentiment remained. If Joey betrayed the code of omertà by squealing about the family business to outsiders, he burned in hell. Kid Blast was left out in the cold, to shoot stick at the Longshore Rest Room with the nobodies.

Larry strove to get in the good graces of the Don, Giuseppe "Joe" Profaci, a man to be emulated. After humble beginnings in Villabate in the province of Palermo and quitting school at fifteen to sell olive oil with his father, Salvatore, the Don had become America's largest importer of olive oil. As the FBI wrote in their files, Profaci was "greatly respected by men of the church, men of politics and government, and men of business and industry."

Rather than applaud the Don, senators summoned him before the Kefauver Committee. J. Edgar Hoover branded him a "Top Hoodlum." The IRS demanded $1.5 million in unpaid back taxes.

The Don refused to pay. He looked to where the soft sands of Bath Beach once were, only blocks from his formidable two-story brick home in a four-lot compound guarded by a high iron fence. The beach had been paved over by a highway. Money to government was wasted, be it Roman, Byzantine, or Bourbon. Not like the tribute paid to Don Vito Cascio Ferro, that great man of confidence from Profaci's days in Palermo.

Everyone prospered under Don Vito. Even the beggars in the street counted on his protection. All gave tribute in respect to Don Vito. It was not the extortion demanded by Il Duce, who plunged Italy into the anarchy of war. A year before Mussolini took power, Profaci stowed away on the SS *Providence*, leaving behind the Mediterranean for the shores of America, bringing with him only the honored ways of tradition.

Over the years, as America fought the Italians, Germans, Japanese, and Koreans, Profaci obtained macaroni and spaghetti factories in Jersey City, a stake in a famed Brooklyn brewery, and footholds in the garment and shoe industries. But it was his vast olive oil holdings—the Santuzza Oil Company, the Mamma Mia Importing Company, and the Sunshine Edible Oils Company—that earned Profaci his nickname, the Olive Oil King.

The Don gave his brother Frank a management position in the Mamma Mia Importing Company. Salvatore, his younger brother, received a stake in the PLS Coat and Suit Company. Sal led a comfortable life, with two racehorses stabled at Lincoln Downs and a large boat docked in Sheepshead Bay— until it was blown up in an accident, may Sal's soul rest in peace.

After adopting Sal's daughter as his ward, the Don threw

her a lavish wedding reception at the ballroom of the Sheraton Astor, overlooking Times Square. Tony Bennett crooned
love songs celebrating the day, which sealed the bond between
the families of Bonanno and Profaci. For his own daughters, the
Don spared no expense. He married Rosalie off to the Zerillis,
a fine Detroit family with interests in horse racing. His other
daughter's hand went to the Tocco Family. Her dowry included
the packing company that shipped Carmella Mia Olive Oil,
named in her honor.

The Don gave the brunt of the spoils to his sons, who
lounged on the lawn of the Profaci compound, shaded by its
well-manicured trees. They received the choice cuts of the family business. "Nest eggs for my little chickens," chuckled the
Don, who smoked big cigars while sitting stiffly in his high-
backed red leather chair. Truly the Don was *uomo di rispetto*, one
who exacted respect at a glance. When forced to resort to
harsher means, he relied on the Gallos.

Like any father in the 1950s, Profaci was concerned by that
plague brought on by the jukeboxes, juvenile delinquency.
"Could this happen to your boy?" asked *Look* magazine in its
profile of "Brooklyn's Teen Thrill Killers." It happened to
Junior Persico, the youngest made man of the Profaci Family. Short and scrappy, with bug eyes and bushy eyebrows,
Junior looked a bit like Dean Martin in a certain light. Polite
and well-mannered, he seemed innocent as a choirboy, but his
teen gang, the South Brooklyn Boys, were among the toughest of the city's sixty-five antisocial gangs.

At a fair one Friday at midnight in the summer of 1950,
five South Brooklyn Boys duked it out against five Red Hook

Tigers at the rumbling grounds near the mall at Prospect Park. The rule was fists only, until switchblades flashed. All thirty rumbled in a brass knuckle free-for-all. Someone pulled a revolver and shot a Tiger dead.

"Is this Junior's old man?" Detective Bartels would ask on the telephone.

"This is Carmine's father," replied Mr. Persico.

Carmine Persico Sr. was at a loss. A stenographer at a prestigious Manhattan law firm, he had raised his family in a nice home on tree-lined Carroll Street in the good part of South Brooklyn. He expected his son to make something of himself. Instead, Carmine Jr. dropped out of school and became Junior, picked up on a murder charge after a dock sweeper was found dead in the Carroll Street gutter. The charge was dropped. Word on the streets was that Junior's older brother, Allie Boy, took the rap.

Eluding hard time at only seventeen, Junior got scooped up by Frankie Shots, who saw the promise of a future all-star. Shots put him to work running numbers with Larry, who mentored him in the trade, but whereas the Gallo brothers went the way of jukebox extortion, Junior found his genius in jumping onto the running board of a truck and flashing a gun in a driver's face.

"Junior used a Luger," said Detective Bartels. "Don't let anyone tell you different." Informants stated that Junior packed two guns at all times. Junior was made a man before he was twenty-five.

Working on Fifth Avenue in South Brooklyn, Junior had a tough crew, including the father of his godson and a big half-Scot bodyguard called Apples McIntosh. In the summer of 1959, Junior pulled off a flawless job on an Akers Motor Lines truck coming out of the terminals by the Gowanus Canal, scoring a $5K payoff on $15K worth of cheap linen.

The Don demanded a third of the take in pizzu, a tradition from feudal Sicily, when men on horseback roamed the sun-baked estates of Palermo, protecting peasantry from bandits in return for a scoop of grain, enough to wet the beak. It was Profaci's way to keep his sons in line, to keep the wild ones from, as they said in the old country, taking a step further than their stride. The Don's moneyman, an illiterate Sicilian gambler called the Sidge, collected the pizzu and made the delivery in a grocery sack.

Hidden under the fruit and vegetables was a ripe chunk of greens from the Gallo jukebox racket, $1,800 from Junior on the Akers job, but nothing from the $2.4 million policy bank of Frankie Shots.

Everybody dove for cover, scrambling for the booths of the dimly lit tavern. Wood chipped off the blasted door. Frankie Shots staggered in and dropped. His Stetson fedora lay beside him on the sticky floor. He tried in vain to get up and say something to the shooter, but there was a hole in his throat. His head thunked back. He stared up at the nicotine-yellow ceiling.

The black-and-white bubble tube above the bar announced next week's episode of *Wagon Train*, Ed Wynn playing a riverboat captain who escorts his orphaned grandson to Arizona. The ad man came on, selling Maytags and Brillo Pads, all that Frankie would miss out on once he was dead. The roly-poly gunman removed the .38 Smith & Wesson from Frankie's camel-hair coat pocket, knowing exactly where he kept it, and emptied a final bullet into Frankie's eye.

By the time Deputy Chief Inspector Raymond Martin arrived on that cold November day in 1959, Frankie Shots lay dead on the floor with eight holes in him. Nobody saw nothing, not even Cardiello, the tubby bartender. Cardiello said he'd been glued to *Death Valley Days* on the tube. All Martin could get was that the two gunmen wore tan topcoats with matching red scarves wrapped around their faces and brown fedoras pulled down over their brows.

Martin rounded up the usual suspects, but to him, the work bore the mark of one Joe Jelly, "a fat little torpedo who reminded me of Mae West," said Martin, "except that he suggested deadliness more than sex." The tabloids called Jelly "The Enforcer." His official police description was "swarthy." He had a fierce rep as the chief gun of the Gallo brothers. He did good work. Neither he nor the brothers reaped the rewards.

Instead of giving the Gallos the $2.4 million policy bank of the late Frankie Shots, the Don gave it to his brother-in-law, the Fat Man, beer king of Brooklyn, who every morning covered his enormous gut with an oversized white polo shirt and stuffed his bulk into his riding breeches to ride his white horse across the twelve acres of his East Islip estate.

"When you want somebody hit," complained Joey, "we're good enough. But not good enough to come to the house."

Not once did Old Man Profaci invite the Gallos to sit at his enormous mahogany table for Sunday spaghetti dinner. His latest snub was a bitter blow for thirty-two-year-old Larry, who bet the Gallo stakes on the promise of dirty work equaling future gain. The greatest Gallo holding was still that greasy spoon, Jackie's Charcolette.

The Gallo brothers had gotten up in the world since the days they ran a floating crap game in the backroom of Jackie's, but Umberto still had to sneak two or three dollars out of its cash register every evening. Mary still had to flip burger after fifteen-cent burger.

Larry didn't get any of the great rewards he expected after being made a man in the Profaci Family. The Old Man wouldn't give him his due.

In March 1960, the Gallo brothers, their top gun Joe Jelly, and Junior Persico sat at Piers, a South Brooklyn bar and grill. Like many revolutions, theirs fermented over a few drinks. The boys were mob stars, credited in the underworld as the legendary Barbershop Quintet, but all were stuck at the bottom rung of the Profaci Family. Save Kid Blast, who hadn't even gotten the courtesy of getting made. The quintet took the risks, busting hump on the mean streets. The Don took the money. And while pizzu worked for peasants in thirteenth-century Sicily, in the New World citizens took up arms against unfair taxes to a mad king.

The quintet plotted a coup against Profaci, but Larry knew it was impossible. Even if they knocked off the old man, the underworld Commission would never approve the Gallos as the new heads of the family. Coups had been pulled off before, but only from men on the highest levels, politely stabbing each other in the back or waiting until they eased into the barber's chair. The Gallos were just the guys who pulled the trigger.

Subterranean

Music was Joey's passion since the day his grade school teacher, Mrs. Lowenstein in classroom 3A, let him come over to her house and wind her Victrola. "Beautiful music. Such a wonderful thing," remembered Joey. Years later, at the start of the swinging sixties, he sat in his glittering nightclub, the Arpeggio, and skulked at the B-lister on his bandstand. The tired horn of "Sweets" Edison sounded like it'd been dragged out of a Harlem nursing home. The place was sour. Joey needed new kicks fast. Ali Baba stepped in as his sworn protector.

The Egyptian bodyguard could crack ribs with a running head butt and freeze his dark features into a terrible mask, striking terror in a victim. "I only have to sit and stare," explained Baba, "and I scare him this way." Traveling the world in stints of forty days and forty nights as a cook for American Export Lines, Baba told stories that laced his hash, reputed to be the best in Greenwich Village, with the mystery of ports afar. At hash parties, Baba would sit cross-legged with a bandana around his forehead and puff a hookah until the room filled with smoke.

Baba turned Joey onto hash, teaching him to chew it like a plug of tobacco, but felt it was best for Joey to smoke communally, in a vibe conducive to connections. On a wintry night in February 1960, Baba led Joey up the four flights of stairs to a pad in the Village, to meet a close friend, Al, a former waiter at the San Remo, the coffeehouse on the corner of Bleecker and MacDougal streets.

The Remo was the hangout of the beat generation, from novelist Jack Kerouac to poet Allen Ginsberg, a place to rant on the conformity of the Eisenhower era and hold espresso-fueled arguments on whether Cuban rebel Fidel Castro was hip or square. The notoriously nasty waiters served up drop-dead looks to the Subterraneans, a collection of beatniks who sat in the wooden booths under the pressed-tin roof and downed rounds of martinis, a cheaper drunk than beer. No love was lost between the Remo waiters, local boys from Greenwich Village, largely Italian, and these beat invaders of their turf. Particularly thick-looking with jet-black hair, a barrel chest, and a menacing jaw, Baba's friend Al served round after round of martinis, but couldn't help overhear the beats quote dog-eared copies of *The Rebel*, by French existentialist Albert Camus. Al submerged.

Caught up in the cultural upheaval, Al put it all on the line to live the life of an artist. He now sat by his California blonde wife, Joyce, at the sparsely furnished Village pad of her best friend Jeffie, dark-skinned with a black beehive to match her curves. Baba introduced Joey to the room. Jeffie made the connection.

"There was a kind of instant energy exchange," Jeffie said of her unexpected guest. "I can't explain it. His electricity was vibrating in the air."

"The random course is altered," Joey would write of their star-crossed love, "its pounding rhythm is altered, its pounding rhythm increases, deafens and explodes! Showering the cosmos briefly upon passing comets, zooming past brilliant stars, touching Venus, then descending slowly, dizzily, in a spiral, the souls are fused—the Latin beat returns—kiss and expand, the world and universe you command."

Jeffie put a jazz record on the hi-fi. Joey told her to drop by the Arpeggio sometime. She showed up in paint-splattered dungarees. The headwaiter stalled her as a blonde got whisked from Joey's table.

In light of the latest B-lister, Monty Babson, billed as "the Frank Sinatra of Britain," Joey split with Jeffie to a dive on the West Side, Lucky Pierre's, advertising "superb French specialties cooked to order by blowtorch magic." The tiny candlelit backroom was freezing since Lucky hadn't bothered to deal with Con Ed, but Joey and Jeffie huddled on the over-stuffed couch and listened to Joyce sing torch songs before the grand piano.

"He felt it," said Joyce, "in a way that isn't usual, except among musicians." Joey became a regular at her gigs, a time for him to take his hands out of his pockets, unclench his jaw, and feel loose.

At Jeffie's pad, Joey smoked cigarettes, drank coffee, listened to jazz, and argued the meaning of life. He was heavy into Nietzsche. Jeffie was absorbed in the banned books of the late Dr. Wilhelm Reich, a Village favorite. A philosopher healer, Reich argued that Fascists propped up father figures in order to reinforce mass repression. "It was the first time Joey had ever discussed things like that with anyone," said Jeffie. The couple rallied on to the cause of society's ultimate orgasm, a life explosion that Reich predicted would overthrow the Little Man in sexual revolution. The pad heated to a crucible of jazz and sex.

The night of Joey's hung jury on jukebox extortion, Jeffie threw a beat-the-rap party at the Arpeggio. Bobby Short was back, offering farewell ditties to the great nightclub years. Tables cleared to make room for Horace Diaz's Latin band, and everybody danced the cha-cha. *The New Yorker* called the scene mad, saying, "this old candelabra shop is nursing a split personality," missing the hip point of it all. Downtown in the Village, mad was happening, in mad pads at mad parties.

Raves for *Dinny and the Witches*, a swingy musical at the Cherry Lane Theater, claimed, "Mad, Man! But Quite Good!" Cabaret act Lambert, Hendricks & Ross sang *Twisted*, the tale of a schizophrenic chick who tells her jive analyst that two heads are better than one. The mad haircutter of Sixth Avenue—"He is mad!" raved Henrietta Hairdo—snipped within earshot of the mad ladies locked up in the House of D, who catcalled passersby on the street to come up and show some love.

Stark raving mad in a goatee, playing a big string bass, Charles Mingus howled down jazz dens from the Half Note to the Open Door. At the Village Vanguard, Mingus ate raw meat backstage before his set and ripped a door off its hinges, furious that the marquee had read "Charlie." Some mad cat kept the door as a souvenir. When the band didn't swing, Mingus decked his trombone player on stage. No time to wait for the music. Mingus needed it now.

So did Joey.

Mingus checked into Manhattan's gothic Bellevue Hospital, the safest place to hide from an offer he couldn't refuse, a personal management contract by Crazy Joe.

Joey decided to make a go for it in the Village. He took up painting, like the abstract expressionists brawling at the Cedar Tavern, a few blocks from the pad. His portrait of Jeffie burst with animal energy, an uncanny likeness painted completely from memory during a brief stint at Rikers Island. Joey was clawing his way up from the bottom, unlike Jeffie's first husband, jazz icon Gerry Mulligan.

Jeffie was practically a kid, bouncing around the Hermosa Beach jazz scene, when Gerry had come to her table at the Lighthouse, the launching pad for the West Coast Sound. Having hitchhiked cross-country with his enormous baritone sax, he asked her if he could buy her a cup of coffee. Jeffie thought Gerry was Christlike, Kerouac's word for all Subterraneans, for whom nothing mattered but breaking past the barriers to Go! Gerry went there. Jeffie married him.

In practice sessions in a house in Watts, Gerry and his matinee-idol-handsome trumpet player, Chet Baker, blew it out in telepathic chemistry. "I had never experienced anything like that before and not really since," said Gerry. Then the LAPD nabbed his hot new sound on a dope raid. Gerry took the rap for Chet and got six months on the honor farm. Chet left the Gerry Mulligan Quartet for good. Crying at the police station, sick and tired of her husband going as low as he could go, Jeffie split for good.

Jeffie found work as a Hollywood press agent but began to get migraines. She broke down in front of a lunch date. He offered to help.

They flew out to New York to spend the weekend with Dr. Albert, a genteel Southerner trained in the controversial teachings of Dr. Reich. Jeffie learned that she stifled her natural rebellious urges, blocking the proper flow of her life force. According to Reich, deep orgasm—vaginal, not clitoral—shattered blockages and restored flow with the universe. Left unchecked, her migraines could turn into cancer.

Jeffie was ready to break her deep-rooted fear of freedom, but a press agent's pay wasn't going to cut it. Heading to Vegas to work the Strip as a sequined, feathered showgirl, Jeffie learned the Reichian truth. Society was sick, chain-smoking slaves to the slot machine. She made enough to pay for Dr. Albert's treatment. Therapy left her deeply attached. "Dr. Albert was Daddy," she said.

Joey filled the void when Daddy packed off for California. Jeffie never thought she'd end up with a gangster, but when it got down to it, all Subterraneans wanted to be gangsters. Ripping off underworld argot, they called each other "daddy-o" as if their fathers were bootleggers instead of insurance salesmen.

Freewheeling in love on a long Village stroll, Jeffie recognized that lanky surfer blond on the other end of the block. Gerry. He was in town, playing at the venerable jazz den, the Village Vanguard. He looked down on Joey, turned to Jeffie, and said, "You must have scoured the gutters of the Village to find somebody lower than a jazz musician."

For Jeffie, it was a compliment. Gerry killed his genius with dope, leaving his eyes like busted television tubes. Joey burned bright and blue.

Jeffie canceled her treatment with her new Reichian therapist, Dr. Bruce, and left the breathless message: "I am getting married and going South." The kickoff party was at the Copacabana nightclub. White plastic palm trees stood stiff as Copa Girls shook it in mink panties. Joey's mother, Mary, fixed a steely gaze on Jeffie, dancing close to her Joey on the ballroom floor. Mary called Jeffie "the gypsy whore." She couldn't even cook.

The couple wheeled out of New York City, escaping the frigid, ice-chunked Hudson for the open road. Used to being chauffeured, Joey watched out the window as, behind the wheel, Jeffie crisscrossed Route 1. The road cut south to Virginia and dropped down through the Carolinas. Neon vacancy signs lit musty rattraps. Morning brought coffee and cigarettes at greasy spoons. Gas station attendants pumped fuel in the crude sucker and checked out the odd couple. Joey smoked down a Camel. The blacktop burned. Palm trees reflected in his big shades, welcoming him to the Sunshine State. Joey told Jeffie to pull over to the gas station. He stepped out of the car and headed for the pay phone.

The bride-to-be was ready for Miami, where they'd find a justice of the peace and begin life. No circumcision on the baby, insisted Joey, and no pinching. Joey hated how his family pinched babies.

Jeffie simply wanted a "nice, free human being that came from both of us, free of all the shit that we'd been stuffed with." She only wished she understood the times when Joey pulled back, why he would put one of Baba's records on the hi-fi, Arabian music with pipes and drums, and stare out of the window, looking past the city in a trance. "I knew that he was sad," said Jeffie, "but I knew I couldn't help him or even go near him. There was something that had to be done. I have no idea what, but it had to be done alone."

Revolution

Tony Bender warned Joey not to marry that ex-showgirl. Best keep her as a Village mistress, like the chic brunette, a sportswear designer for professional skiers, who Bender stashed in a luxuriously decorated three-room pad on Sixth Avenue. A month-to-month rental. Exciting. Creative. Not the marrying type.

Weeks before the shotgun-wedding road trip, on a wintry December night in 1960, Joey strutted down Mulberry Street, lined with dented metal garbage cans, alight with red and green Christmas lights draped above. The smell of almond holiday pastries wafted from Ferrara's Italian Bakery. A neon crescent moon illuminated the Luna Restaurant. A jolly statuette wearing a chef's hat waved from its storefront window. Wingtips clacked across the black-and-white tiles as Joey crossed under the pastel fresco mural of a simmering pink Mount Vesuvius and into the backroom. Old Mama Luna watched over her waiters. Tony Bender made sure Joey got the royal treatment: choice cuts of steak, the best wine, and a regular table. Bender took a liking to Joey, a young man with spark who was making a go for it on his turf.

As the boss of Greenwich Village, Tony Bender offered top protection for the jazz clubs and coffee shops that sprang up in the Village, all for a quarter of the profits. For every sixty-five-cent eggcup of cappuccino sipped in defiance of the system, Bender got his nickel and dime as the biggest profiteer off the beatnik invasion.

Professorial in a mohair suit, the aging Bender looked at Joey through his horned rims. He lifted a shot of espresso with his upturned pinky. A diamond-encrusted ring flashed inlaid sapphire.

Having offered his wisdom on Joey's personal life, Bender moved onto business. A player in the backstabbing underworld, always on the right end of the knife, Bender encouraged the Gallos to take on their Don, Joe Profaci, a beetle of a man, ripe to be squashed.

Instead of the all-powerful Oz of South Brooklyn, Bender saw a frail old man hiding behind his high iron fence, rich off the pennies he shook from his own men. Bender promised to use his powerful connections on the underworld Commission to back the Gallo brothers, the missing link in their quixotic plan to take over the Profaci Family. It seemed an act of lunacy, a .90-caliber big shot backing button men like the Gallos. Then again, Tony Bender was the boss of the Village.

In blitzkrieg raids across South Brooklyn, Larry dispatched members of the Gallo gang, traveling in limos, to kidnap those closest to the Don—his bodyguard, Colombo the bookie, the capo of Red Hook, and the Don's brother Frank. But when a limo pulled up at the Don's Bath Beach compound, the Don wasn't behind the high iron fence, cigar smoke trailing from his red leather throne. He wasn't at Twelve Pines or even at the winter villa in Miami Beach, a sparkling haven where the

Sicilian could dream of orange-scented Palermo during long afternoon naps. The Gallos got everybody but the one man they needed.

The Florida sun beat down on Joey's mole. He walked away from the pay phone and came back into the passenger seat. His face turned into a death mask, pinched around the sockets. Jeffie asked him what was wrong. Joey jumped down her throat. She drove the uneasy stretch to Miami.

For three nights, Jeffie lay under the itchy motel bedspread. Joey burned as if he had caught a tropical disease. Afraid to say anything, Jeffie slipped out, called a friend in the Village, and told her, "I've got to get out of here. I've got a fucking maniac on my hands."

The news on the botched coup was enough to ruin Joey's wedding plans and give Don Carlo Gambino another heart attack.

On doctor's orders that he spend the winter in a warm climate, Don Carlo and his wife were staying at the Palm Beach Towers Hotel. It was too risky to call an emergency meeting of the Commission, but four dead hostages would be a St. Valentine's Day Massacre for New York City. Too hot, especially in the wake of that embarrassing gaffe in Apalachin. On behalf of the underworld body, Don Carlo decreed that his fellow Don, Profaci, address the Gallo grievances and arrive at a settlement on one condition: no violence.

Larry kept his cards to his chest so as not to appear too anxious, but planned to let loose the hostages and squeeze old man Profaci for three bowling alleys, a bigger piece of the action, $150 Gs for past hurts, and the $2.5 million dollar policy bank of the late Frankie Shots. A shrewd bargainer, Larry might even get it. Larry loved to negotiate. It brought out the businessman in him.

One day, when the old man was dead in his grave, Larry could be the new don of the Profaci Family. He'd grow old until he wasn't any more use to the Commission. The next Murder, Inc. would probably whack him off in a barbershop when he didn't have any more hair.

Joey stared out from the Overseas Highway, a hundred and fifty-nine miles of concrete stretched across the Florida Keys. Old farts about to croak gawked at paradise. The blue seascape was littered with condos. This was what Larry wanted, a nice spot on the ocean to retire. Jeffie breezed past islands of wild orchid trees.

Sweat bubbled up on Joey's brow. The road continued on to its end at Key West, leaving ninety miles of ocean until Cuba. Jeffie hit the brakes and wheeled around, back to the pink death of Miami. Joey had no way of knowing that there, Old Man Profaci lay in an anonymous hospital bed with tubes stuck in him, dying of cancer.

"If anything happens to me," said Joey, "I want you to go with my mother. With the kid."

"I'm not having a kid for your mother," said Jeffie. "If you want your mother to raise a kid, go fuck your mother."

The shades were drawn tight in four of the hundreds of rooms at the enormous French chateau-style Manhattan Hotel on

Madison and Forty-second Street. Two Gallos guarded each hostage.

The Don's brother-in-law, the Fat Man, clutched his chest and cried out for his nitro pills, for his bad heart. Joey wanted to gut him, dump him on the old man's doorstep, but Larry wasn't budging.

If they touched a hair on a hostage, Profaci would come after the Gallos with everything he had, an underworld army two hundred strong and a deep war chest. Joey didn't care. He screamed his guts out at Larry like when they were kids. Larry slapped him. Joey stormed off.

—◦◦◦◦◦—

In the midst of a blizzard, Joey showed up at Al and Joyce's West Side apartment looking for Jeffie. She wasn't there. Only Al, Joyce, and Jean, a friend of Jeffie's from Vegas. Joey offered her a lift.

Jean had kept her distance from gangsters since her days with Gabe, a Dead End Kid who was friends with Ali Baba, who once froze up Jean in a Brooklyn diner by leaning in close and asking, "Who is that ripe little, plump little, innocent little *plum*?"

The snow fell heavy. Jean figured a ride couldn't hurt.

The car careened down Bedford Street to Jean's pad in the West Village.

"I could use a drink," said Joey. "Why don't we go to the bar on the corner?"

Jean was tired and ready to climb into bed, but figured she'd be safe at the corner bar, Guido's place.

Guido poured the brandies.

Joey confided in Jean things he said he'd never told any-one else, like how he had based his life on *The Prince*. Jean dug the parallels between Joey and Machiavelli. They even looked alike, she said, "except for their coloring." One drink turned to two.

Joey burned with the manic, nervous energy that bubbled through his being. "Couldn't get over it," remembered Jean. "Looked like a gangster, talked like a poet." After a while, she eased up, thrilled to talk literature with someone who actually read. Jeffie would always ask Jean, "What is he talking about? What does he mean?" Jeffie didn't read anyone but crackpot Reich. Jean was really beginning to like this guy. She knew something special was happening, as though they'd been brought here together, in this storm, for a reason.

"Why don't you paint? Why don't you write? Why don't you get out? Do what you want to do. Paint. Sing. Dance. Per-form. Write. You're an artist. What are you doing?"

"Jean, Jean," said Joey.

They knocked off a whole bottle of brandy. It was one in the morning. They'd been here for hours. It hit Jean. The poor driver was stranded in the car, probably snowed over by now.

"Don't worry about him," said Joey. He paid the tab and they split. "Oh! Look at that. My driver left."

"Oh, did he really?"

"Yes. And I've no place to go. Do you mind if I come down to the house?"

Jean brewed coffee while the blizzard raged outside her win-dows. Her cat Bianca curled up beside Joey. He hadn't made a pass all night. Jean handed him a mug.

"Where's Jeffie?" asked Joey.

"I've no idea," said Jean. "Not the slightest."

Joey pulled a gun on her. "If you don't tell me where Jeffie is, I'm going to kill you."

Jean was a little tipsy. "I'm not going to tell you. So why don't you just put that thing away and drink your coffee."

"Then I'm going to have to kill you."

Jean laughed harder this time.

"I don't know who you are, but Jeffie is a very dear friend of mine, and I'm not going to tell you where she is, okay? So if you'd like to kill me, go ahead. I have no family. No one's going to miss me except Bianca, my pussycat, and I'll be out of this vale of tears."

Joey put away the gun and slept on the couch with Bianca.

The Sponge

The heavy gulped his coffee at his suite in the Sheraton Towers in Chicago. Bellhops brought in breakfast. On his way to be reelected to another five years as Teamster president, Jimmy Hoffa sat with his nattily dressed insurance man, Allen Dorfman, and felt his blood pressure rise. No longer the punk kid counsel for the McClellan Committee, the little monster Bobby Kennedy was now the second most powerful man in the United States with the Justice Department at his disposal. Hoffa got the creeps, convinced he was the victim of a Bobby plot involving electronic beams and invisible tracking powder rubbed into his seersuckers. Hoffa cracked his knuckles for round two. He was all worked up on how Bobby got away with painting truckers as racketeers. Not a single employer in the trucking industry came forward in protest, leaving it up to the Teamsters to defend American free enterprise against the Kennedys.

Hoffa downed more coffee, jacked up like a Mack truck for today's speech before four hundred trucking executives at the eighteenth convention of the Local Cartage National Conference.

The telephone rang.

"Jim, we're coming up to see you."

It was Hy Powell, a bug-eyed union rep in the New York City jewelry biz, hot about a meet. He called all over for Hoffa, trailing him from DC to Pittsburgh before catching up with him in Chicago. Hy flew in on the last three seats on a red-eye from Idlewild in New York City, bringing along Mr. Herschlag and Mr. Rubenzal. They were all down in the lobby, which was crawling with detectives, another arm in the Bobby plot.

"Fine, come up, and have breakfast."

"I already had breakfast. I'll be up in three minutes."

Hy stepped in with an Arab and a little twitchy guy with a big mole on his face. Joey stuck out his hand, knowing a big guy like Hoffa could tell a fella by his shake.

"Jimmy turned ash white," one witness put it, "and ran into the next room."

<hr />

In this day and age, it wasn't paranoid to be paranoid. Joey could dig it, especially when you were getting poked by a ramrodding attorney general. Everybody was paranoid about conspiracy. Nobody knew who was in charge anymore except for Joey, sitting next to Ali Baba, checked in as Herschlag and Rubenzal on the return flight to Idlewild. Joey looked forward to the day when he and Hoffa could kick back and laugh about what had happened over a highball.

Hy Powell didn't take Hoffa's rejection so well. It gave Hy

second thoughts about the corporation he set up with Joey to insure union welfare pension funds, a scheme mastered by Allen Dorfman, the man who sat in the Hoffa suite. Hoffa let Dorfman handle the insurance for the Teamster Welfare Fund, from which Dorfman stole tens of millions in pension dollars to spread around the underworld. Hy hated slamming the door shut on a potentially lucrative deal.

"I loused myself up completely, just by walking in the room there," Hy told his pal, regretting that he brought in a notorious gangster like Joey unannounced. "When you come in, he wants to know who you're with, and he's got a right to know. Hoffa has a right to know. Cause I don't know what's going on. This is right before a convention where the man had a billion dollars at stake, and here I walk in, and perpetrate somebody on him that he may or may not want to see. It's a terrible thing."

Joey had gone on and on to Dorfman about wasting eight hundred dollars on car and airfare to see Hoffa, small potatoes to guys with billions at stake. "You don't play with big people like that," Hy scolded himself.

One of the boys in Hoffa's suite planned on using Hy for a big liquor-industry drive in Florida and California. Hy hoped to move his family to Florida on account of the deal. Now Hy was stuck in New York, owing five hundred dollars to a two-bit check casher, Teddy Moss, who operated out of a second-floor umbrella shop in the fur district.

"How's business?" asked Hy.

"Not too bad," said Teddy. "But general conditions around stink."

Teddy was having problems collecting from deadbeats. Hy got the picture, knowing Teddy hadn't called him up to his umbrella shop to ask about his health. Hy wanted Teddy off his back, so the next day, he came back with Sid Slater, Joey's front man.

"Hy tells me that you run into problems sometimes," said Sid.

"Once in a while," said Teddy. "Most of the time I do manage to straighten it out."

Sid offered a truckload of hijacked liquor for Teddy's bar interests, a steal at only $48,000.

"Where do I have forty-eight thousand dollars?" asked Teddy.

"Are you kidding? Well, if you can't handle it, handle a third."

"I can't handle anything."

Fifteen minutes later, Sid returned with a former linebacker for New Utrecht High School and Joey Gallo—collar up, shades on. Joey picked a few objects off the desk, checked for wires, and gave Teddy a frisk. Teddy thought he knew Joey from somewhere. It hit him. Teddy and his friends used to go to Jackie's Charcolette for fries and Cokes. Those were good times for Teddy.

"You made me a hamburger once or something!"

"Come on downstairs with me," said Joey.

They took the stairs down to Twenty-sixth Street. Joey walked Teddy over to Eighth Avenue on this warm May day and explained, "These are friends of mine. You got to do right by my friends. You should do the best you can for them and you won't be sorry. What are you going to do with my friends?"

Teddy felt his blood drop to his feet. He read about things like this.

"If there is anything you want to know about anything," said Joey, "I'll tell you. Anything you want to know. I'll tell you. You want to know who murdered this guy, that guy, anything."

"I don't want to hear anything, I don't want to know anything. Leave me alone."

"You're smart. You're twenty-eight. It's better that way. The less you know the better off you are."

Joey split to the luncheonette for coffee. Back at the office, surrounded by his colorful umbrellas with polka dots, Teddy told the linebacker to take a hike. He wanted to talk to Sid alone.

"Sid, what the hell goes on here? Who are these people? Who sent for them? What are you doing to me? Who told you I got forty-eight thousand dollars? Who told you I got twelve thousand dollars? Who told you I need any of this stuff? Who asked you to bring them? I don't want to get involved with these people. I don't want to get married to them."

"You're not our type," said Sid.

Sid left to give Joey the news.

"This kid is a wise kid," said Joey. "He knows his business and we're going to have to show him that we mean business. We'll go back upstairs and I'll take the ball. We'll put on a little act."

Joey took his troupe back to the umbrella shop. He sat, put his chin on his hands and stared at Teddy silently for ten minutes, snatched an umbrella handle and banged it on the desk, then picked up a book and flung it at Sid, his own front man.

"Why'd you bring me to a dud like this!" shouted Joey.

"For Christ sake," said Teddy, "who told you I got this kind of money? I don't have it. I owe on a car, a mortgage on the house, a million and one things. Look at how much money I owe. All I do is owe money." Teddy opened four of his loan books for proof.

Joey got up from his chair, looked Teddy in the eye and asked, "Who do you think the city is run by? Guys like you? Or guys like me? We control the city."

"Joey's mad," said Sid, shook up after getting the book thrown at him. "He's going to bang my head off! Do something. If you can't go for twelve thousand dollars, just go for eight and a half. To show that you want to do right by them, try and get five hundred dollars. You got five."

Teddy knew the score. Forty-eight thousand dollars to five hundred dollars was a big drop. All they wanted was a transaction. Teddy knew enough to know you never made a transaction.

Teddy confirmed with Mike up in Kew Gardens. A big, affable guy with a wife and kid, they used to call him, "Mike of Queens." Mike told Teddy not to worry. He said that he checked out Joey's rep. They called him Crazy Joe, but really Joey was just a small-time punk trying to grab what he could and make a big name for himself. Teddy figured as much. Anybody who flipped burgers behind the counter for his mother couldn't be that big.

In exchange for the tip, Mike told Teddy he wanted a fur coat wholesale for somebody's uncle. Teddy brought up an armload of pelts to the umbrella shop on Monday morning. Mike rifled through them, deep in fur when Sid walked in to collect that five hundred dollars.

"Go see Hy, who gave me the big buildup and the big send-off," said Teddy. "Tell him to go jump in the East River."

The next day, Teddy got his biannual haircut at the Dawn Patrol on West Fifty-fifth Street. The barber was just brushing him off when in walked Joey with the linebacker. Teddy watched them head straight for the chairs in the back of the barbershop. He figured it a coincidence. He paid his bill and tried to duck out.

"How ya doin', buddy?"

Teddy froze. Joey was smiling in the mirror. His bib was on. His muscle sat in the chair beside.

"Did you take care of all the checks? My friend is getting a haircut too."

"No, I didn't."

"That's not very sporting like."

Teddy said he was going out to get a paper. Hurrying across the street to his car, he tossed in a thick envelope and slammed the trunk. He looked up and saw Joey, waiting in front of the Dawn Patrol. His bib was off. His hair was uneven.

"Let's walk," said Joey.

Joey walked Teddy up Broadway, against the midday hustle and bustle. Gray flannel suits, hair slicked with Brylcreem, hurried back to the office. At the end of a long day, they'd head to Grand Central to catch the five o'clock train. Too busy to pay any attention to two strangers, one close cropped, the other half cut.

"This is a big city. A lot of strange things can happen to wise guys. As we are walking now, a brick can fall on your head, you can fall down a cellar, or a car can run you over."

"I'm not a wise guy," said Teddy.

"Don't lie to me. I got you pretty well checked out. I admire you. You're an ambitious kid."

"I don't know who you got your information from or who checked me out. I have nothing."

"Keep your voice low," hissed Joey.

A man in a hat passed.

"You got to watch where you're talking. That's a detective.

Didn't you see the bulge in his pocket?" Teddy didn't. "Until the heat blows over, I'm going to be leaving town, and I want to know, before I leave, who my friends are and who they aren't. I want to remember you as a friend. Don't you want to be my friend?"

"I have nothing to be your friend with."

"I know that you put an envelope in your car."

"Yes, I did."

"Why did you do that?"

"It was an envelope and I wanted to put it in my car."

"If you were in my place now, what would be the next question that I would ask me?"

Teddy thought a second. "Let me see the envelope."

"That's right. I want to see that envelope."

"It's my envelope. I don't want to show it to you."

"Now you got me thinking. Before my mind was a million miles away. I had you built up. I had you pegged for one thing. Now I don't know how big you are, how much you got. Now I'm beginning to think that God-knows-what can be in that envelope, and that isn't good for you. If you were smart, you'd show it to me so my mind can be relaxed."

"Look, I don't know what you want. But I'm in a hurry. I got an appointment and I got to leave. I got to make a phone call because I'm late already."

Teddy stepped into a phone booth. Joey waited and walked Teddy back to his car.

"Well, how are we going to leave it? Are we going to leave friendly or otherwise?"

"I don't know how we are going to leave."

"Okay, pal."

Joey gave Teddy's hand a shake. Teddy got in his car and drove the hell off.

Later that night, Joey sat at his table in the backroom of the Luna and asked the boys about Mike, the hefty player at the umbrella shop who was trying on fur coats.

"Who could this Mike of Queens be?"

"I don't know," said Sid. "The only thing that I do know about Teddy Moss is that he has a place called the Rumpus Room in Queens and this fellow might be out there. It would only be a wild guess, but what we could do is make a phone call over there and find out."

The linebacker stuck a thick finger in the rotary hole and called the Rumpus.

"Yeah, they have a Mike there."

"Boy, we're good detectives," said Sid.

"Call again," said Joey, "and tell this Mike that the boys downtown want him to come over to the Luna Restaurant, and want to know how quickly he can be here."

Mike arrived around the same time the late-night hookers rolled in. He didn't want any part of that, not like nine years ago. Mike used to be a lover. The women used to go for him. He lived off them, them and the track. But after one too many afternoons of waking up beside some broad, Mike wanted a Maytag.

"What are you," asked Joey, "strong-arm man?"

"What you mean, a strong-arm man?"

"You're making a hundred dollars a week and you want to be a hero."

"I don't want to be no hero. I'm through being a hero nine years ago. I want to make a living. That's all I am making, a living."

Joey told Mike he'd fit him for a wooden kimono—a coffin—unless he got Teddy on the phone and made him come to the Luna.

Teddy got dressed, but his wife, Ethyl, wouldn't let him out of the house. Teddy got back in bed, under the covers. After Ethyl fell asleep, he crawled down to the basement phone. Ethyl caught him up. Teddy was back in bed when Mike called to ask what was taking so long.

"Ethyl is up, and she knows about this and she's hysterical, and she won't let me go!"

Mike held the phone from his ear as the boys smoked, drank, and ogled the hookers. "He can't make it tonight. His wife knows about it. Can he make it some other time?"

The next afternoon, shortly after one o'clock, Teddy and Mike sat in front of Joey inside the sparse backroom of the J&A Card Club on a side street of Little Italy. Joey had on a black suit, black shirt, and white tie. He smacked Teddy across the face with an open palm.

Teddy tried to get up but was smacked again. His eyes were bloodshot. His face puffed up. He lifted up his hand in defense. Joey smacked him.

"What are you, getting smart? You want to hit me or something? Now, ask me, 'Why am I a wise guy?'"

"Why am I a wise guy?"

"Because you got your friend Mike into this thing. He had nothing to do with it, and you got him in a jam. Now *he* is in it."

"I didn't get nobody in."

Joey smacked him. "You better smarten up."

Joey left Teddy and Mike alone with Ali Baba, who was sitting in a breezy silk suit, staring his terrible mask. Joey came back after ten minutes. He pulled up a chair next to Teddy and laid it straight. "If it wasn't me, it would probably be someone else. I got a lot of people to feed. There a lot of people like me that have to eat. All right, c'mon, let's go out and get some coffee. Then call your wife, tell her everything is all right."

The next morning, Teddy laid out his sob story in Room 1101 of the Prince George Hotel on East Twenty-eighth Street, tricked into thinking that the two clean-cut undercover cops sitting across from him were gangsters who could put the squeeze on Joey.

Teddy cringed. He wasn't the type to blow whistles. Nor was his father, Charlie, sitting beside him. Teddy had come to him with a puffy face, spilling his guts about his problems with Joey.

"He was scared to death," said Charlie.

"Scared to death, right?" asked Detective Romaine. "Did they threaten anybody else in your family?"

"The only thing he said," said Teddy, "was that he wanted to make an appointment for tonight and I said my wife is nervous and all that and he said, 'Who's the man in the family? If you can't handle her, I'll go talk to her. You pay the rent, you tell *her* what to do.'"

"I honestly don't believe he's in danger," said Charlie. "This slapping around is definitely to impress."

Detective Romaine introduced his superior, Lieutenant Vitrano of the NYPD Rackets Bureau Squad, saying, "He has been in Brooklyn I say more times that he's been in New York. Why? Because the fucking *Gallos* come from Brooklyn." Romaine was ready to take that prick Joey and give him the stretch. He handed Teddy a lineup photo. Teddy stared at Joey in black-and-white.

"After a while, it gets to a point," said Teddy. "What I would like to do is go down there with a gun and see the two or three of them, blow their brains out, and run."

Romaine worked the angle. "You go out and work like a son of a bitch, and building up a business and your bars and grills and your check-cashing business, and some guy operates the door and declares himself—what did he say to you? I'm a partner, did he say that?"

"Yeah. I'm a *partner*."

"Hello, partner."

"He starts that way," said Lieutenant Vitrano. "You wind up on salary in the end and then you wind up out completely."

"How do guys like this get away with it constantly?" boomed Charlie.

"They don't get away with it constantly. I've personally stopped them a few times and he can be stopped."

Romaine went for the kill. "We talked like people here, like sensible people give up their lives fleeing Europe, being subjugated to fucking dictators. And they give up their *lives*. You're reading the Eichmann thing. Gave up their *lives* because they believed in something. I don't want you to be a hero. Don't look at it that way. You're just ordinary people. Here's an opportunity to take this guy and take him for good and all those other scums that are with him."

Teddy didn't want to end up like the sad case of Arnold Schuster, an innocent pants-presser and amateur crime-fighter who went to the police after recognizing the infamous bank robber fugitive Willie Sutton on a street corner in Fort Greene. Willie got sent to Attica. Schuster got paraded around the television like a hero before Murder, Inc. gunned him down in an alley.

Teddy called up Mike for advice.

"I don't know what to do. It's a mess."

"The best thing to do is, Teddy, don't say nothing to nobody."

"No, I ain't saying nothing to nobody but—"

"They are very big. They hit the tops . . . Where are you?"

"I just got out of the office. I wanted to think it over. I was thinking of taking it on the lam, running away."

"Suppose you did go on the lam, where would you go? You got your home and you got your business, and stationery, you lose everything. You lose everything."

"So you lose everything."

"And what have you got? Use your head . . . They will grab you. You know that."

"Suppose they do. How far will it go?"

"I don't know. I don't know."

"Will they go as far as killing me?"

"Jesus, I don't know. I don't know."

"Yeah, but they got me down there. They might smack me around."

"No, it's a restaurant. Teddy, the best thing is the truth. You can never hide from the truth. The truth is the truth. You can never get away from it . . . Coming right from my heart, Teddy, from my heart. My mother should rest in her coffin if I am kidding you."

"Let me ask you something? Is there anybody that would go see . . . to get these guys off my back?"

"No, Teddy."

"I thought they were so small."

"I thought so too."

"Why couldn't it die over?"

"Because it don't die, Teddy."

"No, they brood more and more."

"Where you going to go to, to Europe? They will get you in Europe."

Teddy wished God could get him out of this. Mike nipped that idea in the bud too.

"God? Nobody is God. God is dead a long time ago."

That night, at two minutes after seven, Teddy arrived at the Luna, which was guarded by a lookout pacing back and forth outside the front entrance on Mulberry Street. Teddy checked out the backroom and stood about nervously with his hands in his pockets. He returned to the narrow front hallway and sat in a cramped booth with a white tablecloth, right under the palm tree painted above on the mural. Joey strutted in wearing a fedora, black suit jacket, and white shirt, unbuttoned at the collar. Mike followed.

Joey eyeballed a good-looking waitress—"Hello, Mama!"— and motioned to the back, saying, "I don't want to talk no business until we've had a feast. Let's go to the rear where we'll have more room."

Teddy walked under Mount Vesuvius. Joey chatted up the bartender and paid respects to Mama Luna. The waiter offered several good bottles of wine—Chianti Ruffino at four dollars a bottle, or Asti Spumante at six dollars and fifty cents. Mike tasted. Teddy didn't want to drink anything. He sipped his water.

"Go ahead, have something," said Joey. "You'll feel better. They have good steak here. It's nice when everybody has a buck in their pockets. It's good to eat steak. It's not good for anybody to go hungry. What do you think, Mike? Live and let live?"

"Yeah."

Joey turned to Teddy. "Don't *you* agree?"

"I believe in live and let live, let everybody go out and work for a living."

Teddy picked at his shrimp cocktail. Mike and Joey dug into steaks. Both agreed the food here was much better than in the joint.

In the middle of the meal, Joey and Mike headed into the kitchen. The cooks chopped garlic, poured in the olive oil, and stirred the rich sauce. Teddy felt the heat on the back of his neck. The whole place seemed to be in cahoots with Joey except for the three undercover cops sitting behind Teddy. They looked out of place. They looked like cops. Joey and Mike came back and polished off the steak, enjoying every bite.

"Joe, I don't want anything to do with this thing. My wife is hysterical. She's scared."

"Did we go through that yesterday and we have to go through it again?" snapped Joey. "What gives with this kid? What is he, stupid? *Se ha bisogno di un po' di tempo per pensarci, lo mandiamo in ospedale per quattro, cinque mesi, giusto il tempo per pensarci.*"

"Take it easy," said Mike.

Joey stormed off.

"They are awfully annoyed," said Mike. "They are not fooling around. You know what he said to me?"

"No."

"That if you need some time to think it over, they'll put you in the hospital for four or five months, and that'll give you some time. Listen, Teddy, I spent nine hours with these guys last night. They are not kidding."

"I don't know."

"Look, I just want peace. I had enough of this nine years ago. I just want peace."

Fate had sucked Mike away from the clean life. Now he would live dirty. He would wake up late, go to the track, and live off women, and felt the best thing for Teddy was to throw in the sponge too.

Joey came back and called for the check.

"Did your *wife* know you were coming down here? The place is crawling with cops."

Joey's boys, stationed throughout the Luna, sprung into action. One ran into the kitchen, grabbed a waiter's jacket, removed glasses and dishes from the tables, and slipped off. Mike followed Joey onto Mulberry and waited for Teddy, who walked out and headed in the other direction. Mike grabbed his arm and pulled.

"Come on," said Mike. "Everything is all right, I'm with you."

"Mike, I'm not going down that way."

"If he don't want to go," spat Joey, "just leave him."

The cops came in for the kill. The bartender ran out at the commotion.

Mike had just enough time to spin around and hand over a big bill roll, which the bartender relayed to a waitress. She tossed it in the freezer box and slammed the door shut.

Absurd Deaths

Leaving Jackie's Charcolette on the back burner, Larry head-quartered the family business, the newly incorporated Direct Vending Machine Company, in the storefront of 51 President Street, a three-story brick tenement owned by his Grandma Nunziato, right at the edge of the Red Hook waterfront. Having negotiated with the Vendall Company in Glen Cove, New York, manufacturers of pre-mix soda machines, to be their distributor in South Brooklyn and Long Island, Larry at last had the monopoly on teen rebellion, from the nickels plunked in the jukeboxes down to the sugary sodas sipped idly in the malt shops.

Everything was set to make that transition into big business, to leave behind the life of a small-time gangster for good, but Joey couldn't give up the Udo act. He threatened to set the family back a few decades by putting the shakedown on Teddy Moss, a real nobody who didn't even know the reputation of the infamous Crazy Joe. The crime could land Joey fourteen years in the joint. Mary had to mortgage her Flatbush home in order to post the $15 Gs in bail. The Tombs was no good for her Joey. It made him jittery. His hands shook when he shaved.

To raise the $25 Gs for his lawyer fees, Joey gambled a chunk of money from his union insurance scheme but came up short. He tried to borrow from underworld sources but could only scrape together fifty bucks. Larry was in no position to help.

After the NYPD got tipped off on the coup against Profaci, eight detectives dubbed the Pizza Squad took over a vacant apartment on President Street across from Gallo headquarters. The squad kept a close watch on Larry, making it tough for him to conduct business. He was so stretched thin on cash that he couldn't maintain the mortgage payments on his home. The repo man snatched his car.

By order of the Commission, Old Man Profaci was supposed to come to a settlement with the Gallos, but Larry still hadn't seen a cent of that $150 Gs the Gallos demanded for past hurts. Both parties were negotiating through John Scimone, a "used-truck dealer" who served as the Don's trusted bodyguard and chauffeur, valuable enough to be one of the hostages held at gunpoint during the coup.

After six months of an uneasy peace and no breakthrough in negotiations, Scimone called Larry and said he had some good news. Larry decided to meet him alone. His top gun, Joe Jelly, was off on a dirty weekend with his girl on the side after a deep-sea fishing trip in Sheepshead Bay.

Larry put on his black jacket and porkpie hat and drove the loaner to a South Brooklyn street corner for the meet. Scimone was middle-aged, with thinning black hair. His long face was unusually cheery after a big day at the track. He forked over half his winnings as a good-faith token. Larry snatched up the crisp, folded-over C-note, trying hard not to look desperate.

"Let's go to the Sahara Club and have a drink on it," said Scimone. "Some of the boys will be there."

Larry drove Scimone to the Flatbush cocktail lounge and pulled into its small parking lot shortly before three. The Sahara wasn't supposed to be open until six on Sunday due to the city's blue law. It was a Profaci hangout. Larry followed Scimone in through the side door. It was dark inside. The Doberman wasn't there, only the tubby bartender, Charlie Brown, polishing glasses by a dim bar light. A diamond stickpin twinkled from his tie.

Larry knocked one back.

Scimone drank up and took a leak, leaving Larry to stare at his moon face in the mirror behind the bar. The surface was murky, covered under years of grime and cigarette smoke, or maybe being a Gallo brother had simply taken its toll on Larry.

Hands emerged from the dark glass out of nowhere. Larry saw the reflection of a manila cord as it looped around his neck and pulled tight. He scratched at it but his fingertips slid off. The rope twisted tighter, expertly pulled at the knotted ends. The garrote ripped back and forth across Larry's neck, sawing into his flesh, slow and methodical. Larry fell off the stool onto the floor.

Always neat as a pin, he hated that everything spilled from his bowels. His heart stopped.

<hr />

The Eighth Street Bookshop was a haven for sanity in a world gone mad. On the pages of the *Evergreen Review*, paid for by ads from the Fair Play for Cuba Committee and the Russian Tea Room, the little magazine showcased the best of the counterculture, including chapters from Jean Genet's prison epic and poems by Lawrence Ferlinghetti—"You're whirling around in your little hole Fidel and you'll soon sink in the course of human events."

Hiding the bestsellers on the bottom shelves and showcasing insane poet Ezra Pound behind the enormous display windows, the haunt for Village literati drew in a range of wanderers, from weird cowboy Jack Palance to strange gangster Joey Gallo, checking out the fiction.

"I read a lot of Camus," Joey told the clerk.

In a bad omen to kick off the decade, the French novelist and philosopher Albert Camus was killed instantly on January 4, 1960, riding shotgun when his publisher swerved off the RN5 south of Paris and smashed his Facel-Vega into a tree.

"With the death of Albert Camus we reach a point of dying," mourned Howard Hart in his *Village Voice* tribute entitled "Camus: The Right Side of Our Face Has Fallen Off." "Camus saw that even though everything might be destroyed, we must face the endemic hypocrisy in Western Man, we must expose it . . . *Camus did expose the lie.*"

"See, my father must have really instilled on me," comic Lenny Bruce riffed on the mike, a Village favorite ranting in underworld argot, "there's nothing worse than a lie. Yeah sure, all of us, that's our generation, 'There's nothing worse than a lie. Just don't *lie* to me.' . . . So apparently my father wrapped it in solider than other people. So when I see the lie I don't want it to *be* that way. You said that. *Do* that. Be the judge. And *cool* it. Don't get out of your cug completely."

"I can prove my innocence if I am able to get out into the street and get my witnesses together that are necessary to prove my innocence," Joey promised the judge in regard to the Teddy Moss case. "There is a lot in this case that is underground, and I think the district attorney is being hood-winked by a smart operator. Through the squeeze, not knowing me, he put me into this swindle, your honor, and I can prove it if I am just given a week's time to get out into the street."

Once he was freed, Joey was too busy to go underground and fix the trial. He needed to find his proper place in life. "After all," said Lenny Bruce, "there's nothing sadder than an aging hipster."

Jeffie caved in and married Joey after he threatened to marry a nice Italian girl. Jean the cat lady was the bridesmaid. Baba was the best man.

"What are you doing with that terrible man?" asked Jean.

"Come on, Jean, leave him alone," said Joey. "This is my friend, my uncle, my father."

Baba filled in for all who didn't show. The Gallo family didn't approve. "Everybody disapproved of the whole thing, including me by this time," said Jeffie. Two days after her City Hall wedding, she was pregnant again, having lost her first baby in the wake of Miami.

Grandma Nunziato listened to the news as she sat in her room on the second floor of 51 President Street, headquarters of the Direct Vending Company. "One look at her," wrote columnist Jimmy Breslin, "told you that you were in the presence of greatness." Silent in old-country black, her iron-gray hair pulled back tight, Grandma Nunziato, or Big Mama, as the tabloids dubbed her, paved the way for Jeffie's entrance into the family. Her daughter Mary would have to love the gypsy whore.

Jeffie was out the door for a Sunday visit at her sister-in-law's when she realized she'd forgotten her present, an electric teakettle. Joey made her go back with him to get it. At five-and-a-half months, it was getting hard for Jeffie to schlep her baby belly up the four rickety flights into their record- and book-strewn pad. The telephone was ringing off the hook. It was for Joey. Somebody at the Sahara. Joey picked up. A voice on the line croaked, *"You're next on the list."*

⌇⌇⌇⌇⌇

The last person to identify Gallo triggerman Joe Jelly was his wife, Mrs. Jelly, who watched him waddle out the door with a black coat, black tie, and a white shirt over his squat body, covering the scar on his left shoulder. He looked as good as he'd ever look, ready for his upcoming dirty weekend in the country with his woman on the side. Jelly kissed the missus and stepped out of their Bensonhurst home. It was a scorcher, a dog day in August. The papers said the humidity was "one point below the level where almost everybody should feel un-comfortable."

Jelly slid onto the fine-grain Florentine leather of his gray Cadillac Imperial sedan with a big dent on the side. The AC cranked. The Imperial rode like a dream, keeping an even keel over the potholes.

Jelly passed Randazzo's on Emmons Avenue, where Don Carlo Gambino enjoyed the finest calamari and red sauce in the five boroughs.

Jelly rolled off the leather seat of the Imperial, felt the breeze of Sheepshead Bay, and headed to the thirty-two-foot-long cabin cruiser of his Marine buddy and crap-game part-ner, Sally D, a chesty hulk who owned a little fruit stand on Avenue U.

Jelly looked out to the vanishing strip of land, leaving behind the heat, the wife, and the best calamari and red sauce in the five boroughs. Jiggling with the waves, he breathed in the gasoline and fish smell as they trolled the open water. It was a great day to go deep-sea fishing. Somebody opened a frosty one from the cooler.

The boys on the cabin cruiser chopped up Jelly, cut off his arms and legs, removed his innards and stuffed the gutless torso in a barrel. They threw it overboard into the bay. According to informants, the barrel floated back up. They weighed it down further until it sunk. Jelly's gray, dented Cadillac was cut up at an auto parts store on Boston Road in the Bronx before getting crushed in an auto wrecking lot in Milford.

Next on the hit parade was Larry Gallo, and it all went according to plan. Sally D squeezed the life out of him, twisting the manila cord with the length of metal pipe, sawing it back and forth across the neck in the painful tradition of the Italian rope.

Junior Persico allegedly watched.

In the aftermath of the strangling, two members of the Gallo gang sat in a sleazy hotel, trying to figure out why Junior slunk so low as to set up Larry for the Shanghai at the Sahara. Junior and Larry knew each other since they were kids, running numbers under Frankie Shots.

"They put their arms around each other, they love each other. They are big buddies."

"It's wonderful to love another man. It's wonderful to walk away."

"Well, that's when you put the knife in, you know. When you get close to somebody."

The act of betrayal earned Junior a new nickname in the underworld, the Snake.

Nobody called him that to his face.

For Junior, the nickname capped off the end of a tough summer, rough going after a rat in his crew on the Akers job squealed in Federal Court, landing him a guilty verdict on hijacking interstate commerce. Thrown into the Federal Detention Center on West Street, Junior was released on $25,000 bond before his sentencing. According to an FBI informant, Profaci capos Johnny Bath Beach and Jiggs Forlano approached Junior and promised he'd be made a "boss" of Brooklyn if the Gallos disappeared.

Junior was halfway there when Larry's heart stopped on the Sahara floor. A flash of light cut into the bar as the side door creaked open.

"How are things?"

"Everything is fine, Sergeant," said the bartender. "Everything is great."

The NYPD sergeant heard a low moan on the floor.

"Take him!"

"Not here! I don't want trouble here."

The gang rushed out but didn't expect a patrolman in the parking lot, sitting in the prowler in broad daylight. Sally D pulled the snub-nosed revolver from behind his trousers, shot the patrolman in the face, hopped into the getaway car, and sped off onto Utica Avenue.

Inside the Sahara, now brightly lit, red returned to Larry's blue face. He blinked his eyes open to a group of officers, squatting over him.

"The bastard," groaned Larry. "The dirty bastard. He gave me a C-note. He gave me a C-note."

GANGLAND TALE:
THE NOOSE THAT FAILED

New York Post
AUGUST 21, 1961

At the Snyder Avenue Station, Inspector Raymond Martin of the 76th Precinct in South Brooklyn tried to get Larry to fess up on who strangled him and shot the patrolman lying in fair condition at Kings County Hospital. All Larry would say was, "Nobody would want to do a thing like that to me, Mr. Martin."

Joey glowed next to his brother. "He's clammed up," he bragged to the gang. "He's not saying nothin'." Picked up at his Village pad, Joey was on high alert after Larry phoned from the Sahara and croaked, "You're next on the list." Joey couldn't stop staring at that deep purple welt dug around his brother's neck. "Gallo will carry the scar from the rope burn to his grave," said Deputy Inspector Alfred Panarella. The patrol car dragged Larry and Joey to the DA's office. Larry looked out of the window, lost in the distance. A burning cigarette dangled from Joey's lip. He stared right into the *Daily News* camera when the shutter snapped shut.

"They are birds of a feather, denizens of the underworld," said the Kings County judge. "They won't talk. They're going to settle it their own way, under their own rules. You can expect other murders." The judge held Larry in $100K bond as a material witness in his own strangling, but cut Joey loose, reasoning, "I cannot commit him just because somebody says he will be the next to be attacked." Turning to Inspector

Martin, the judge ordered, "The only way to break the back of the underworld is to shadow its members night and day. Drive them crazy."

Outside the headquarters of the Direct Vending Machine Company, Joey laid down the stakes for the Gallo gang, twenty-five men strong, armed to the teeth and ready to wage an all-out war against the Profaci Family. The Don had an underworld army of two hundred men, superior in firepower but inferior in spirit.

Outmanned, outnumbered, and clearly in over their heads, the Gallo gang would pull out all of the tricks to annihilate as many Profacis as possible. The gang kissed their wives goodbye, packing them off to distant relatives, and grabbed mattresses. Fifty-one President Street became the Dormitory, a fortified compound to match the Alamo. The gang nailed chicken wire behind the windows to bounce off grenades. Digging in for the long haul, Umberto Gallo commandeered the mess on the second floor, stocking the shelves with soda and cans of tomato paste, stuffing the fridge with fresh mozzarella and strings of sausage from the local *salumeria*. The gang filed down the points of the .30-30s for the John Wayne special, the Winchester 94. They loaded the magazines of the M1 Carbine high-precision military rifles and lubed up the Mossberg and double-barrel J. C. Higgins shotguns.

Gallo sentries stood silent on the three-tiered, tarp-covered Dormitory rooftop. Locals had been warned to keep off the streets. Some boarded shop, but most stayed, loyal to the boys and ready to alert them of danger. Outsiders didn't stand a chance in this tight-lipped neighborhood, silent as a Sicilian village.

A full moon arose over President Street, setting the stage of the showdown in Red Hook, South Brooklyn's concrete-cracked Wild West.

Junkyard dogs roamed the colorful cargo containers on the shipping yards. Derelicts lay passed out underneath the Brooklyn Queens Expressway. A car cruised silently past Jackie's Charcolette at two-thirty in the morning. A package flew out of the back window. Inside was the last outfit of Joe Jelly, wrapped around several dead fish. Lying at the bottom of Sheepshead Bay, Joe Jelly slept with the fishes.

```
URGENT   8-23-61   10-25 AM
TO DIRECTOR, FBI
FROM SAC, NEW YORK
JOSEPH GREGORY GALLO AKA, AR.


INFO RECEIVED TEN PM AUGUST TWENTY-TWO
LAST, THAT JOSEPH GALLO HAD GATHERED A
LARGE GROUP OF MEN IN VICINITY OF VAN
BRUNT AND COLUMBIA STREETS, BROOKLYN. MAY
HAVE THOMPSON MACHINE GUN. GALLOS HAD
WARNED INHABITANTS OF AREA TO KEEP OFF THE
STREETS.
```

On the FBI tip, Inspector Martin ordered his men, nicknamed Martin's Marauders, to barge in on a midnight raid. Shadows moved across the rooftops toward the Dormitory. Raiders ran up the creaky narrow stairs to the second floor and flicked on the light, revealing Joey, Blast, Chico, and Lefty, sitting around a linoleum table.

"What are you doing sitting in the dark?"

"We were talking," said Joey. "What's that, a new crime?"

Bringing in floodlights, the raiders looked under furniture, behind the doors, and into the closet, where they found a box of .45s and Vinnie the Sicilian. They'd expected twenty-five men armed with Tommy guns, but the Gallos wired up a makeshift network of intercoms and walkie-talkies, buying plenty of time to hide.

According to an FBI agent, during police raids, the Gallos jumped out the rear Dormitory windows and shimmied down hanging ropes and ladders into adjacent buildings. Paths of entry and escape lay throughout the rubble-strewn back lots, from the third-floor apartment at 31 President to the entire building at 75 President. Hideouts and stash houses for the arsenal were up and down this single block of President Street.

The only weapons found in the raid were two double-barreled shotguns lying on the rooftop, unconcealed and perfectly legal.

The boys spent the night in the rat-infested Raymond Street jail, and at noon were brought before Flatbush Court on consorting with criminals, each other. "We arrested them," said an officer, "because we didn't want to find bodies all over the streets. It was building up to open warfare like in the Roaring Twenties."

Free on bond, Joey strutted down the stone steps of Flatbush Court. The cuffs of his white button-down hung loose, half rolled up and unbuttoned. Mondo the Midget trailed behind.

On Monday evening, August 21, the Gallo gang spilled onto the sidewalk of Mama Rosa's Italian restaurant, sat on the curb and swigged wine from the bottle. Joey threw his brother an epic welcome home from the joint and survival bash.

"What'll happen now?" asked a guy in the gang.

"You don't think Joey and me are gonna take this lying down, do ya?" croaked Larry, a scarf tied neatly around his neck, covering his weak spot.

Back at the Dormitory, Larry roused snoozing Gallos, snoring open-mouthed in crumpled clothes, half-sprawled and stinking hungover on eight mattresses laid out on the third floor. He ordered all clothes hung neatly on long wood racks, military barracks style, and all cigarettes extinguished in sand-filled cans. He took a record from his vast opera collection and cranked it. The clang of metal and the male chorus of *Il Trovatore* fired up the troops. The music rang on President Street.

Unable to lock up the Gallos for good, but not wanting a massacre on his watch, Inspector Martin ordered the Pizza Squad to guard the eight-block radius around the Dormitory with 24-7 surveillance on the Gallo gang. "Without our protection," said Martin, "their lives would not have been worth a counterfeit subway token."

Inspector Martin called roll every morning to ensure Kid Blast, Peanuts, Punchy, Joey T, Vinnie the Sicilian, Sammy the Syrian, Louie the Syrian, and Big and Little Lollypop had survived the night.

Detective Bartels got friendly enough with the Gallos to join them at dinner, better than the usual stakeout grub. Umberto donned a chef's hat and boiled pasta in his ten-gallon pot for the big eaters, Tarzan especially, a Gallo with waste-management interests. "He could eat two pounds of spaghetti," marveled Bartels.

Detective Lambert watched Joey T, an art student turned racketeer, mix colors on his palette and paint a statue of Jesus, bought at the monument shop down the street. Others passed the time building remote-control model airplanes, practicing yo-yo tricks, and playing jacks on a stoop with neighborhood kids.

Larry played Verdi on his violin. Scraping from the coffers, he gave each of his men fifty dollars a week, enough to grease the wives' palms on Sunday, Family Day at the Dormitory. Mothers brought in baked casseroles and hot plates, promising, "Don't worry, I've never squealed on your father and I won't squeal on you."

Inside the Dormitory, Gallos were getting fat off Umberto's pasta, growing weaker by the day. All the while, Profacis encircled the Red Hook backwaters like sharks in Cadillacs, hungry to break through the police cordon.

"Let's get our guns and go after them," snapped Joey, but Larry wouldn't budge. Cooped up in the Dormitory behind his chicken wire, he played arias on his violin while Joey choked on the bad air, needing to breathe free.

"Let me die in my footsteps, before I go down under the ground," sang Bob Dylan, who'd just begun playing on MacDougal Street. Out in the Village, the new crop refused to be beat. Protest music rang from the Cafe Bizarre, the Commons, the Figaro, and Cafe Wha? Protesting a ban on folk music in Washington Square Park, young rebels in tweed sang, "We shall not be moved" as cops tossed them over the basin rim of the fountain.

Eluding Pizza Squad tails and Profaci hit men, Jeffie picked up Joey and brought him home to their new ground-floor apartment on Eighth Street with a garden in the rear. His mother's lamp hung from the ceiling, shaded in blue and yellow glass decorated by silver filigree. Joey gave Jeffie one hundred dollars to fix the place up with antiques from the Village auction houses. "He loved all the little things I got," said Jeffie. "It just seemed that everything that one of us did turned the other one on." A loaded rifle stood at Joey's bedside. Lepke the terrier lay at his feet. Joey and Jeffie were happy.

"We never discussed the future," said Jeffie. "We had no future."

"In the past couple of weeks," said a police official of Joey, "knowing he's a marked man, he's been swaggering along Broadway with a couple of his hoods, hitting the spots. He's unarmed and he doesn't seem to have a worry in the world. In fact, he's told us, 'My life is one foot in the coffin, the other on a banana peel. But I don't worry.'" Nothing mattered when the dirt got packed.

"What will they see in a book?" asked Joey. "Paper and bullshit." Camus got a shelf at Eighth Street Bookshop. Garibaldi, the Italian revolutionary, got a statue in Washington Square Park, covered in pigeon shit.

The People vs. Crazy Joe

Joey sent a communiqué to the Profaci Family—Deliver Junior Persico to President Street, "Dead or Alive." Nobody responded. True to his new nickname on President Street, the Snake was slippery. Word on the street was that he never stayed in one place for more than three nights, making him hard to pin down for an ambush by the Gallos. "That bum wouldn't stand still for Pope Paul," swore an NYPD intelligence official. "Only a crazy man could think he could shake the Snake."

```
URGENT   9-20-61   9-14 PM   JFA
TO DIRECTOR, FBI
FROM SAC, NEW YORK

JOSEPH GREGORY GALLO, AKA. AR. DAILY TELE-
TYPE SUMMARY.

CARMINE PERSICO JR. IS TO BE SENTENCED
ON SEPT. TWENTY NINE NEXT AND INFORMANT
```

STATED SUBJECT ANTICIPATES HAVING SOME
MEN IN COURTROOM TO DETERMINE IF PERSICO
SHOWS UP. IF SENTENCING IS POSTPONED THE
GALLO MEN WILL FOLLOW PERSICO FROM COURT-
ROOM IN AN ATTEMPT TO KILL HIM AT FIRST
OPPORTUNITY.

On September 29, the judge at Brooklyn Federal Court threw the book at Junior on the Akers job, sentencing him to fifteen years for hijacking interstate commerce. The slick defense lawyers delayed sentencing. The pockets of the Profaci Family were deep enough to throw money at appeals or set up Swiss bank accounts for witnesses for the prosecution. A month was plenty of time for Junior to go out and beat the rap. Sitting by Junior was his codefendant, Joe Magnasco, aka Joe Mag, the guy who worked the phones on the Akers job. Junior was the best man at Joe Mag's wedding and the godfather of his child. Joe Mag was the proud owner of one hundred Gallo peanut-vending machines. He spit on Junior outside in the corridor.

"You're a dead man," said Junior.

A cordon of NYPD detectives surrounded Junior and walked him outside the courthouse. There waited Gallo troops Punchy, Chico, and Nick Bianco.

"You fink," said Nick Bianco.

"Dirty rat bastard," said Punchy.

"You're gonna get your heart cut out," said Chico.

They spit at Junior. Junior spit back. The cops carted him off to the Snyder Avenue Station and questioned him for several hours on Larry's strangling. "You leave us alone for twenty-four hours," Junior later blurted out in custody, "we'd have the Gallos cleaned out."

The NYPD dragged Junior over to President Street and asked Larry if this was the guy who tried to kill him. Larry looked to the ground in silence. The Mafia called it omertà, the vow of silence, but in the old country, omertà didn't mean silence. It meant manliness, that a man in trouble settles matters his way, not the way of the cops.

On the second floor of the Dormitory, Joey T, the racketeer-artist, painted a prophesy in huge scrawling letters across the dining-room wall: *Don't Talk: The Life You Save May Be Your Own.*

```
URGENT    10-3-61    7-08PM
TO DIRECTOR, FBI
FROM SAC, NEW YORK

JOSEPH GREGORY GALLO, AKA. AR. DAILY TELE-
TYPE SUMMARY

INFORMANT ADVISED CARMINE PERSICO JR. CON-
TROLS A BROOKLYN BAR NAMED CHATEAU RUSSO.
ON EVENING OF OCT. ONE LAST SUBJECT WENT
TO CHATEAU RUSSO WITH SEVERAL ASSOCIATES
AND MADE STATEMENT THAT THE BAR WAS NOW
UNDER HIS CONTROL. SUBJECT IMMEDIATELY
REPLACED BARTENDER WITH ONE OF HIS ASSO-
CIATES. INFORMANT ALSO ADVISED SUBJECT
STATED TO HIM DURING PAST WEEK THAT HE WAS
GOING TO DO A LOT OF DAMAGE IN THE NEAR
FUTURE.
```

Joey planned to put the snatch on Ruby Stein, the biggest loan shark in New York City, knowing he would demand a hefty ransom.

Living in a plush Park Avenue apartment, Ruby spent nights on East Fifth-third Street at El Borracho, its signature drink the Nicky Finn. "If you have enjoyed the dinner, the service, and the atmosphere of El Borracho," read the yellow card on the table, "PLEASE DO NOT tell your friends as our seating capacity is limited—The Management." As Ruby stepped out one October evening in 1961, Gallo hoods Big Mike and Lefty grabbed him and tried to drag him into the parked car. Ruby hung on to the canopy pole and screamed. Big Mike and Lefty sped off empty-handed, just before the cops showed.

On October 4, Joey sat in the Longshore Rest Room, edgy and waiting for Profaci big shot Harry Fontana, the capo of Red Hook. That morning, Joey told Fontana to show up for a sit-down on Gallo turf. Joey was ready to tell him who was boss. When Fontana didn't show, Joey pumped up Junior's old sidekick Joe Mag to go out to the College Restaurant, the capo's Brooklyn hangout, and kidnap him by sundown. Larry said to stay put, but Joe Mag sped off in a brown Buick.

As the sun set on Joe Mag, his cousin, Mrs. Tony Shots, made her way up the steps of the BMT Fourth Avenue subway stop against the rush of evening commuters with day jobs. Like the other wives of those on President Street, she'd been wondering when her husband was coming home. Tony seemed worse for the wear on Family Day, especially after Inspector Martin killed the visits of his fifteen-year-old son. "The boy looked at his father as if he were a combination of Paul Revere and Robin Hood," said Martin. Tony figured that if his son spent some time hanging around, watching the sweaty lunks sit around and play pinochle all day, he'd get disillusioned with the life altogether. Martin knew better. If the visits didn't stop, Martin threatened to charge Tony with impairing the morals of a minor.

Mrs. Shots now saw a crowd hovering on the sidewalk in front of the College Restaurant. Standing in a frock, Father Benny Calleja of Our Lady of Peace opened up his little black book and administered last rites. The police drew a chalk line around Joe Mag, lying face down on the pavement. A blood-stain covered his left cheek. "My God," shouted Mrs. Shots, "that's my cousin Joe!"

Gunned down in the course of trying to kidnap the capo, Joe Mag was the first casualty from the President Street en-campment. Shot down, just like his father, some men re-marked. The wives crossed themselves and could only think, "Could've been my husband." Family Day took a turn for the worse.

"Do you think we can live on thirty-five dollars a week?" screamed the wives. "The children miss you! What kind of a home have we got with no father? You can get a job, you bum! You don't have to be a big shot. I want you home, do you hear me? I want you home!"

Another Gallo gang member, Nick Bianco, had his own beef with the men. A Rhode Island bachelor, Bianco rolled up to President Street with a dapper wardrobe hung up in the backseat of his car. "Them slobs in there never had but three-dollar shirts," he complained. "I come in with good shirts and all of a sudden they're all wearing shirts and changing three times a day. Three times! I never heard of top businessmen changing more than twice a day." His wardrobe dwindled to practically nil, Bianco dressed in his jammies and tucked him-self into one of the row of eight mattresses on the second floor. The gang's German shepherd woke him the next morning, barking at the door before the NYPD broke it down with the battering ram.

Lieutenant Kelly suppressed a smile to find his old Marine buddy, the hulking Tony Shots, sitting in his underwear and shades.

Half-awake at the breakfast table, hardly looking up from his coffee, Larry wished the raiders a good morning. Ignored by several shaving Gallos, the raiders seized three kitchen knives, a bread knife, a hammer, and the Mossberg target rifle. Larry suggested they look under the unmade bed for the twelve-gauge shotgun.

Thirteen Gallos rolled into the paddy wagon, taken in on the same old consorting charge. "If we don't keep picking these hoods up and tossing them into Raymond Street jail every couple of days, if we don't keep them off-balance," said a high police official, "blood is going to run through the streets of this town."

"Inspector Martin, you will never know what you stopped," joked Larry, putting his hands to his purple-ringed throat. "We were up to here. We were going to bust out in Brooklyn, Manhattan, Queens, everyplace. Get the whole thing over."

<hr />

The judge arraigned the Gallos as material witnesses for a Kings County Special Grand Jury investigation, called to get to the root of Larry's strangling and the murder of Joe Mag. "It is quite obvious to the court that this is an incipient gang war," said the judge. He fixed the bail at $25,000 for each broke Gallo.

Picked up hours earlier while eating at a Village restaurant,

Joey yelled to a detective nodding off in the courtroom, "How many days you been working, huh? Everybody on the homicide squad is going to wind up getting divorced. You watch."

Walter Buchbinder joined the proceedings as chief investigator of the DA's Rackets Squad, the boys responsible for Joey's extortion setup.

Folding up his subpoena, Joey poked it at Walter's chest and said, "Someday I'm going to give you one of these things. I've had about a hundred from you, and you haven't solved a crime yet." Poaching a blank one from the DA's office, Joey filled it out and handed it to him the next morning as he strutted into Brooklyn Supreme Court for his grand jury appearance.

"Here, Walter, try this on for size."

The reporters howled at the mockery of justice. Joey played up the farce for what it was.

Hiding their faces from the herd of cameramen lurking in the corridor, Mrs. Shots and Punchy's wife were shuttled into the jury room, having been called to testify on the source of their husbands' income. "These girls will have to go on home relief if their husbands aren't let alone to go back to work," Joey told the press.

Ever-present Gabe Pressman put up the NBC-TV mike and asked about the gang war.

"Jesus, they're not murder guns," said Joey, taken aback. "They're hunting guns. We use the guns for hunting deer."

Standing behind was David Price, Esq., representing the Gallos on behalf of their Uncle Joe, Price's partner in the firm. For the past five months, Price had been trying to pin down Joey to work on his defense, but Joey wouldn't give him the time of day, telling him, "That's legal business. Attend to it. Go away. Don't bother me."

Now Price had to worry about thirteen Gallo gang members in civil prison. Old and cranky, the last thing he needed was Joey's mouth mucking up the works. He grabbed Joey by the back of the neck.

"Goddammit, you shut up!"

"Wait a minute, counselor," snapped Joey. "This is my life. Let me say what I want to say. I want the reporters to get the right story. The police are harassing us."

Joey turned to the chief investigator, lurking in the hallway to check out the act.

"Gang war? Dum-dum bullets! You made up a big story about gang war. There's no gang. There's no gang war. There's nothing. You guys are making something out of nothing, and I want to tell the truth."

The six o'clock news broadcast the truth according to Crazy Joe. He riffed on the mike with the snap of a hustler, ad-libbing free-form attacks on the hypocrisies of the age. He took on the DA's political motives. "It's an election year, right? Everybody wants to get in on the act." He spoke about J. Edgar Hoover's obsession with the Reds. "There is as much gang warfare in Brooklyn as there is a dangerous communist party in this country." He took on the terror of the downward-spiraling nuclear situation, as the world rallied to keep the Soviet premier from test-bombing fifty megatons, the largest nuclear bomb to date. "The only guy I'm afraid of is Khrushchev. This fallout business—I think he's nuts."

Price steeled for a coronary with all of the pre-trial publicity drummed up by his client in the weeks before the Teddy Moss extortion trial. A brutal winter on the way, Price decided to hell with it. He flew south to North Miami Beach, to nap on the chaise lounge behind his Pepto-Bismol pink bungalow, listen to the Giants game on the radio, and drive his blue Pontiac to the early-bird special.

—◦III\ ᶜ\IIII◦—

"Have you got a lawyer?" asked the judge in Manhattan General Sessions Court, Part 8.

"No," said Joey.

Going into his chambers, the judge gave Joey a break by calling Irving Mendelson, a top defense lawyer who had made a name for himself by taking on the strange case of the belligerent writer Norman Mailer.

Mailer prophesied that the Hip would rise in a violent, bloody revolution against the Squares. Looking for evidence, he fired up after Fidel Castro, who had waged hit-and-run guerrilla warfare against the crooked dictator Batista from the wilds of the Sierra Maestra, finally stormed the palace gates. At his October 1960 visit to the UN, Castro partied at the ninth floor of the Hotel Theresa, "the Waldorf Astoria of Harlem," on a seventeen-hundred-dollar room service tab of steaks, rum, cigars. A red, white, and blue Cuban flag unfurled outside his suite. Hundreds gathered outside the barricades on 125th Street. One held a placard with a picture of Castro's bearded face, reading, "Man, like us cats dig Fidel the most. He knows what's hip and bugs the squares." Soviet Premier Nikita Khrushchev showed up and kissed Castro on the cheek, turning the hip scene into Squaresville. Mailer, in a fevered state, wrote a letter to Castro that was later printed in the *Village Voice*.

> *You belong not to the United States nor to the Russians but to We of the Third Force. So long as you exist and belong nei-*

*ther to America nor to Russia, you give a bit of life to the
best and most passionate men and women all over the earth,
you are the answer to the argument of Commissars and
Statesmen that revolutions cannot last, that they turn corrupt or total and eat their own. You are the one who can
show the world that a revolutionary belongs to no one.*

He signed it, "Still Your Brother."

Hopped up on years of Reich, jazz, and a steady intake of
pot, Mailer had reached super-sane clarity on the brink of self-
inflicted madness. Shortly after writing his letter, he stabbed
his wife in the gut and the back with a penknife in order "to
relieve her of cancer." After seventeen days in Bellevue, Mailer
was judged sane. His lawyer, Mendelson, hashed out a deal
with the DA and got the famous writer off on twenty-five hundred dollars bail.

An expert at working the system, Mendelson saw right
through the cracks in Joey's case. The star witness for the
prosecution was suckered by the NYPD Rackets Squad, posing as mobsters. The lynchpin evidence was three undercover
detectives at the Luna who listened to a translation of a vague
threat against Teddy Moss, spoken in Italian with no surveillance tapes to back it up.

Mendelson strode into court on Monday morning, ready
to clean house. Joey pulled him aside and laid down the score.

"That goddamned dago judge is never going to give me a
fair shake."

It wasn't true, said Mendelson. He could vouch for the
judge—fair, honest, a lifelong friend.

"You just told me all I want to know," said Joey.

Joey refused to cooperate with his newly appointed counsel. A figure of authority ordained by the New York Bar, praised

by the *New York Times* as "an outstanding criminal lawyer,"
Mendelson felt he deserved better than to get tossed around the
court like a trapeze artist.

"I am the lawyer and I take orders from no one," he told
the court. "I am ready to try the case."

Picking the first juror from the pool, he officially kicked
off the People vs. Joseph Gallo. Joey cornered him outside the
courthouse elevators.

"Mendelson—that's a musical name. And I'm hip to the
tune you're playing. It's my swan song. How can you choose
jurors for me when you don't even know what my position is?"

Mendelson put up a finger as the doors closed, trapping
the lawyer with the reporters.

"He won't talk to me," said Mendelson. "The judge demands that I represent him. What can I do?"

Taking a page from Mailer's defense, Mendelson cooked up
a scheme with Weiswasser, a junior lawyer in the firm of Price
and Iovine.

If Joey would agree to be committed for mental examina-
tion, the trial could be postponed for enough time for Price to
return from Miami and work on a proper defense. Hearing of
the plan in the depths of Sessions Court, Joey told Weiswasser
he'd "throw that bastard Mendelson out the window, and
you're going right behind him."

<hr/>

"He gave me better marks than my own shrink does," bragged
Joey. "Does that sound crazy to you?"

Gene Grove scribbled furiously at the Waverly Lounge,
the bar of the rundown Earle Hotel, thrilled to get the scoop
on the meaning behind Joey's nickname. Al, the owner, had

seen a lot of characters come and go through the Earle: Ramblin' Jack Elliott in Room 312, Bob Dylan in 305, and now Crazy Joe, just another outlaw drifting into the bar, spilling his guts to the *New York Post*.

"I'll bet the papers are out now," said Joey.

The piano player headed out to the newsstand to pick up copies of the dailies that looked to Joey for tabloid fodder, from the *Daily Mirror* to the *Journal American*. There was Joey in the early-morning edition of the *Daily News*, candy for the straphangers.

Joey took Gene over to the Corner Bistro, on Jane and West Fourth Streets. Norman manned the tiny kitchen, simmering the chili, molding handfuls of ground beef out of ten-pound bags, slapping them onto wax patty papers. Bistro Burgers mixed with the smell of whiskey and old wood at this tin-ceiling enclave for bohemians.

Gene sensed how distant Joey's life in Red Hook seemed from life here, talking literature and holding court with bohemians at the Bistro. "Joey loved the Village as only those who move here from some other where can," wrote Gene. "He spoke of his Brooklyn home as someone might speak of Ashtabula."

On the night before the trial, Joey took Jeffie out to dinner in a French restaurant with their old friends, Al the actor and Joyce the torch singer.

"Listen, Joey. Why do you have to go through with this? They're going to get you. Don't you know that? Why don't you just leave? Tonight. You and Jeffie."

"No, Joyce. I can't do that."

"But why not? Why can't you go to Florida or Mexico? Anywhere. Just get away from it. What if it goes the wrong way?"

"Listen, I've no choice. I can't run away. This is what I've got to do."

"But Joey, what have you got to do that's more important than staying alive and staying together, you two? You've *got* something now. What difference does it make where you are? You've got enough money for a ticket. Go. Do something else."

"Too late. It's done. I've got to go through with it."

"Why? What's more important than your freedom?"

—◆◆◆—

"I stand on the Constitution of the United States of America."

"Have you any particular section of the Constitution on which you are standing?"

"I stand on the Constitution."

"On the whole document?"

"Your honor, I refuse to participate in any of these proceedings."

"Do you refuse to answer my question?"

"I have to remain mute, your honor."

—◆◆◆—

"The defense may inquire, if it wishes," stated the Assistant DA, standing with his shoulders hunched and his palms out. Joey wouldn't let his lawyer speak. Mendelson walked out of the courtroom. The judge ordered Joey to be remanded to the Tombs for the remainder of his trial. Weiswasser rose to object.

"Don't bother," said Joey. "He's too prejudiced."

Joey hadn't bothered to call any witnesses in his defense. He didn't say anything throughout the trial except that he refused to participate in the proceedings and would remain mute. He stuck it to the judge just like he stuck it to Bobby Kennedy, refusing to play his part in the dog and pony show, a sham devoid of meaning.

Stuck in the can on the last night of his trial, Joey dug the true meaning of his nickname. Sure he'd been restless after that car wreck in his teens. He'd just cheated death. Why should he waste his life as a slave to the wrench or a stooge to Uncle Sam? He was no crazier than Larry, who had trembled to the point of blackout at Fort McClellan. Doctors at the United States Army Hospital listed Larry's precipating stress as "separation from the family and the mother's illness," enough to make the barracks think he was sissy. They got shipped to a godforsaken South Pacific island for occupation duty. Larry got discharged with a World War II Victory Medal and a thirty-five dollar a month pension for life, payback for sacrificing his nerves for his country. Bobby Kennedy was the crazy one, obsessed with Hoffa's perfume, reacting badly with the bootlegger blood in his veins. Bobby wanted Joey in the nut factory for life. Public Enemy One was just too good-looking, too smart, and too dangerous for seeing the corrupt game.

Joey saw the only truth, to be forged in hot lead at the edge of nowhere.

The Hash

Before he was Sid Slater, front man for Crazy Joe, he was Sidney Slepp, an Iwo Jima veteran with a wife and kid and an honest job working in a jukebox rental outfit. After Joey took over the operation, Sid stayed on at one hundred dollars a week and moved up to managing Joey's nightspots, including the Playboy on the East Side.

"No one is getting hurt by what I'm doing," Sid told his wife.

"Except you, Sidney," she said. She took off with his daughter.

Balding, with a middle-aged pouch, Sid didn't have a problem finding action with the B-girls hanging around the Playboy. His close proximity to the underworld gave him an allure of danger. Then came the night when Joey called him over and said, "From now on, Sidney, you can just call the five of us the Barbershop Quintet!"

Sid went back to his hotel room and gave himself a good look in the mirror. He thought about his brothers for the first time in forever.

Four years later, Sid found himself in a second-floor umbrella shop, trying to con Teddy Moss into buying a truckload of hijacked liquor. Sid didn't get Joey's hang-up on this guy. Teddy was a B-grade nobody, but Joey couldn't let him slide. It was like he wanted to remake everybody in his image. First Sid. Next Teddy. Then the world.

Driving over to the Piers Restaurant on the night of Teddy's shakedown at the Luna, Sid got stopped halfway across the Manhattan Bridge. The cops came at him with guns and hauled him downtown, taking him through the side entrance of the Criminal Courts building on Leonard Street into the DA's office.

Lieutenant Vitrano gave it to him straight. He didn't talk like a gangster, as he had with Teddy Moss. He talked like a hard-nosed cop.

"You've got three fine brothers and two nice sisters who won't have anything to do with you," said Vitrano. "You've lost a good wife and a lovely daughter. And what are you getting out of this life with Joey Gallo and his punks? Nothing."

"You know how it is," said Sid.

"Tell me," said Vitrano.

"Once you get in, you can never get out. You keep thinking that someday you'll make a big score. Then you can take a quick powder, go somewhere, and start all over again."

"No one ever made a big score working for Gallo," said Vitrano. "You think it over."

They gave Sidney a number when he entered the Tombs, a concrete jungle with the lingering smell of urine. Nobody wanted to hear his sob story. He turned his pockets inside out and handed in his one hundred and fifty dollar suit. Sid felt soft and queasy standing naked for the prison hose-down with the hustlers and the junkies. He tried to wash the black smudges off his fingertips. He stepped into his prison uniform, "a gray job that hung on me like a burlap bag."

There was no AC in his cell. It was hot. Sweltering. The bunk had one blanket, springs but no mattress. The smell—he turned to the enormous black man locked inside with him.

"What in God's name is that?"

"You hungry, man? I been savin' that fish sandwich for more than a week."

Candy heard the special knock at two in the morning on her door at the Mayflower Hotel, towering over the south end of Central Park West. The knocks never stopped, even when she was singing or on the toilet. She told her friend to hurry up and lock the door. She didn't feel like going out to watch Sid and Joey take over nightclubs, eating and drinking for free until the cops reported the presence of underworld characters to the State Liquor Authority.

"Joey and Sid go sit in a club for two weeks and it's closed," said Candy. "Now when they're going out in the evening, they both state, 'What place can we close next?'"

Candy wanted to sit in her room and talk about everything. Metaphysics. Psychiatry. *Joey*. If she got the kind of publicity Joey got, she'd be a star in the theater. Sid didn't get any press. Not like Joey.

"Joey was boss in Brooklyn before he was twenty-two," Candy told her friend.

Joey was like a real-life character out of *The Untouchables*. Candy loved that show. At El Borracho, she saw Joey put down a fifty for a tip after a Diner's Club scam where he avoided the bill. She knew when she met him at the Bowl-a-Rama on West Fifty-eighth Street that he was marvelous, full of ambition, with a fantastic mind.

"The opposition is made up of a little group that's power-ful, wealthy, established Italians," Candy explained. "Joey is bigger than they are. Anyway, these people have lost their power, supposedly a lot of it. It's been given over to Joey. And money has been given over, oh God, I don't know how many hundreds of thousands. At one point, Joey was feeding and taking care of seventy-two families. Do you know what that is? To pay for seventy-two families? Rent and food and this and that and clothes?"

Candy's friend wasn't getting how big Joey was. Candy opened up her bedside copy of RFK's *The Enemy Within* at the well-worn crease in the spine. She read aloud her favorite part, about how Joey's mother couldn't understand how her sons had so much money when they did no work. Candy hoped Sid got some of that cash. She didn't want to badger her good old auntie anymore. She already owed the hotel two hundred. She had to pay for vocal lessons, taught by an opera singer who thought she had a very nice voice. Not to mention dance les-sons, new clothes, and a new apartment.

"I have done a lot for them," Candy told her friend. "While they were in the can, I was their contact outside and I ran a lot of errands for them."

Candy looked after Sid like a baby. If he tried to ditch her, she had enough on him to cause trouble. She could always squeal to the cops. If Joey knew about the way Sid treated her, he would not let him get away with it. She told her friend that not many people knew she and Joey had gotten in a fight, but everything would be all right. Joey wouldn't hurt her. She knew too much. If Sid didn't come through, she'd go straight to Joey.

Her friend finally left, leaving Candy to sit around and think. The weeks living in this hotel room seemed to all blend together. She decided to go out to the African Room on Third Avenue and East Forty-eighth Street, a dark cavern decorated with green shoots of bamboo and a giant papier-mâché gorilla. She had a very funny night, a very witty night, and the bennie she took activated just in time, catching her up with the speed of the dancers and Chief Bay, the conga drummer from Dakar. Before she knew it, she was stuck back in the room with Sid.

"You're lying to me somewhere on something," said Candy. "I sense it as strong as I'm sitting right here now. You're either not telling me something or you're lying about something and I don't know what it is, but I would swear on my life right now."

"Where?"

"I sense it so strongly that I would . . . My life I would stake on it. I've never been wrong with this feeling."

"Well, what's the—"

"I don't know. I'm not saying it's bad or good or anything, but I know something is out of place."

"Where?"

"I don't know. *Where?* . . . I just dropped a piece of hash on the floor. Did you see it? A little piece. Did you see it? Isn't it annoying as blind as I am, these things?"

"Girl with too much. Who sent you the pretty flowers?"

"Does that annoy you so much that I worry about flowers every day? I must keep fresh flowers in the house every day."

Sid tried to compensate for her secret admirer by passing her off some swag, a stash of panties, baby dolls, nightgowns, and cotton dresses, which he had gotten for practically nothing.

"So cheap, you got to like it," said Sid.

"What if I don't like the stuff? Then it isn't cheap at all, right?"

Candy could do better from the fat guy in Times Square who sold Bergdorf Goodman stuff to the drag queens for ten dollars. Sid didn't get Candy's fabulous reputation for dressing.

"I'm a perfect ten," explained Candy. "I've always said this. I can't wear a nine. I don't wear full skirts. That's one thing. I only wear a sheath dress. Certain colors I refuse to wear. I'm very fussy about my clothes."

Honest to God, she could die. Sid felt like a real jerk. Candy consoled him.

"Don't be sorry, dear, because you didn't do wrong. In fact, I think it's very sweet of you. Frankly, I'd rather have the money and go shopping with it myself. I think I'd do better picking things out myself, don't you?"

"Do what you want."

"That's right. Don't resent that."

Candy could see she hurt Sid. She tried to be helpful. She was on her way to go meet a photographer from the *Daily News*. If Sid wanted her to, she'd ask about those rumors she heard about Joey.

"I heard a couple of little rumors last night," she said. "I heard something that concerned Tony Bender, that Joey's been stepping out of hand and Joey's been pushing an awful lot of people. That word is *out*. That is the hash. The sum total left."

Sid said that if he wanted to find out what was going on with Joey, all he had to do was drive over to Joey's and ask him.

Sid still had eyes for Candy, petite and blonde, "a soft doll who only weighed about eighty pounds with a copy of *Variety* in her lap," he said, but Candy seemed to think that he was making a million dollars a week. Sid wasn't making enough to buy her a half-pint of perfume.

Sid was barely scraping by after getting wrapped up in the Teddy Moss ordeal, slapped with $10,000 bail on attempted extortion. Worried sick about getting locked up for fourteen years in the can, Sid snapped when Joey confronted him about the hash situation.

"Have you ever mentioned to anyone that you got hash from Baba?" asked Sid.

"No," said Candy.

"You did mention it, because there's a fellow who came back to a friend of Joey's, who heard from a boy that Baba has the best hash in the city, and would this guy get to Joey to get to Baba to get some hash for him. Now all hell has been raised, including my life. I'm in all kinds of trouble over this and the story is all through the Village. My life is in jeopardy and yours isn't particularly healthy either. Your name was mentioned."

Candy needed to light up.

"No. Don't smoke now, please. There's no hash, no nothin' around here. You know how many ears this has gone to? My life is in jeopardy!" Sid paced the room. "Do you know I can get killed for this? Now listen, I've never given you a piece of hash, understand?"

"Yes."

"And there's nothing between us but friendship."

"Yes."

"You never got a piece of hash from this house. I never left it around. You smoked here, you brought some up, but I have never given you any."

The Gallo brothers, Larry and Joey, take the Fifth before the
McClellan Committee on February 17, 1959.
(AP Images)

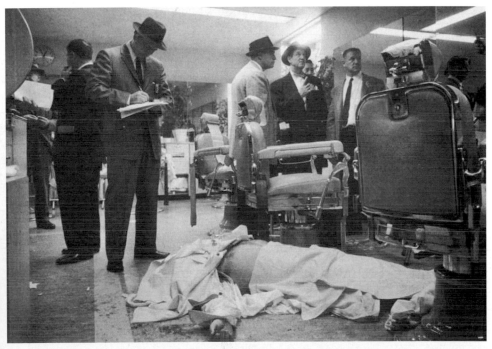

Mob boss Albert Anastasia. Gunned down at the Park Sheraton Hotel
barbershop on October 25, 1957.
(George Silk/Time & Life Pictures/Getty Images)

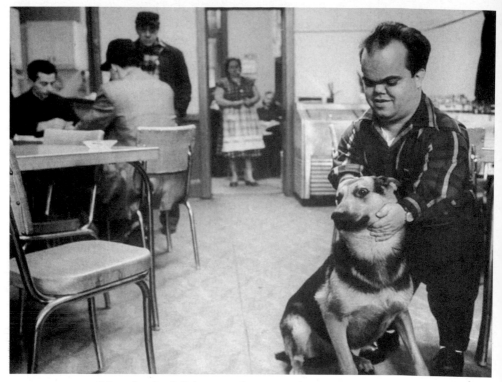

Mondo the Midget at the Longshore Rest Room,
the Gallo gang hangout on President Street.
(Lee Lockwood/Time & Life Pictures/Getty Images)

Gallo headquarters at 51 President Street, aka the Dormitory.
(Marvin Lichtner/Time & Life Pictures/Getty Images)

The Luna
on Mulberry Street.
*(Municipal Archives,
Department of Records
and Information
Services,
City of New York)*

Joey Gallo gets booked for
extortion on May 11, 1961.
*(Municipal Archives,
Department of Records
and Information Services,
City of New York)*

Larry Gallo escorted out of the Sahara on August 20, 1961. *(AP Images)*

Kid Blast, with cigarette, lays it down inside the Longshore Rest Room. *(Lee Lockwood/Time & Life Pictures/Getty Images)*

A few of the boys
pose for *Life*.
*(Lee Lockwood/
Time & Life Pictures/
Getty Images)*

Joey and Jeffie inside a Brooklyn courthouse.
(Lee Lockwood/Time & Life Pictures/Getty Images)

Kid Blast is kissed after the Great Fire.
(Lee Lockwood/Time & Life Pictures/Getty Images)

The boss, Joe Colombo, hands in his pockets, is filmed on the streets
with his son, Joe Jr.
(AP Images)

Joey Gallo with his new bride, Sina, on their wedding day, March 16, 1972.
(Tim Boxer/Getty Images)

Three weeks later, the crime scene at Umberto's Clam House.
(Neil Boenzi/The New York Times/Redux)

At a press conference at NYPD headquarters on April 7, 1972,
Chief of Detectives Albert Seedman watches Police Commissioner
Patrick Murphy point at the diagram detailing the crime scene.
(AP Images)

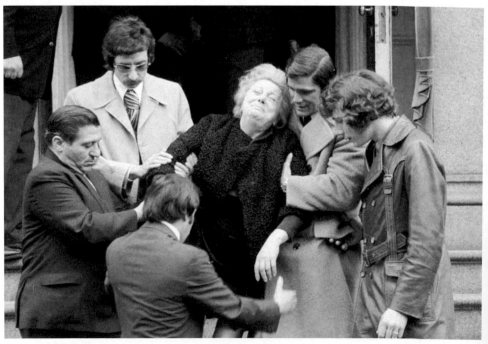

Mary Gallo mourns for her Joey outside Guido's Funeral Home.
(AP Images)

"Yes."

"You have never even kissed me, have you?"

"I'm scared," said Candy. "I don't want to be marked for the rest of my life. Joey is page one!"

Candy tried to get Joey on the phone but couldn't reach him.

"This is serious," said Sid. "You can't imagine how big this could be. It could be a firecracker that would blow up in your face."

"But Sid, baby, I've gone out with these people far more than you know. I love them so much . . . Sid, I love these people. Do you know what love is? How could Joey . . . Joey Gallo."

Candy started to cry. She couldn't believe Joey had threatened to cut her face off for saying he had access to unlimited hash. She'd never act again. No more art movies in Massachusetts or anywhere else. Sid consoled her. He promised to take her to the Palladium and spend the hundred dollars burning a hole in his pocket.

Candy wanted to know how Sid got all that cash. Sid never used to have to deal with these kinds of girls. He was nervous and jittery. He'd lost thirty pounds. Strolling through the Village streets, he heard footsteps and became paranoid. He wheeled around and almost pulled out his gun on a poor girl chasing after her loose Dalmatian. The hash situation hadn't helped his nerves. Worse, Joey was hell-bent on a Profaci killing spree. Larry tried to hold him back, still believing the conflict could be solved without violence, but Joey wasn't listening.

Over the weeks, smuggled in grocery sacks and snuck through the rubble-strewn back lots and over the rooftops of President Street, an arsenal was compiled under the noses of the NYPD. Broken-down rifles ready to be reassembled. Scopes. Silencers. Smoke grenades. M-80s. Bombs. Joey planned to strike on the upcoming weekend, November 18, in an all-out attack against the Profacis, ending it once and for all in a veritable suicide mission.

"Brooklyn was in for a bloodbath," confessed Sid. "I was in a mood to get out if there was any possible way to do it."

It was time to turn in his pinstripes. He ratted out the plan to Lieutenant Vitrano and Inspector Martin. He told them the heavy artillery was stashed in Lefty Big Ears' room on the second floor of the Dormitory. Lefty awoke to thirty NYPD raiders.

Caught in the basement of the Longshore Rest Room with a canvas sack of four revolvers, Umberto was arrested on firearms possession. Eleven in the Gallo gang were hauled in on consorting. The cops missed the big arsenal but stopped the bloodbath. Kid Blast laughed it off, smirking for the *Daily News* cameras in his big sedan. Punchy grinned from the backseat and pointed at flat-topped Butch, smiling wide with his four front teeth missing, knocked out by Joey on one of his bad days. They screeched away from Brooklyn Magistrates' Court.

RAIDS NIP GALLO GANG WAR, SAY COPS

New York Post
NOVEMBER 22, 1961

Across the bridge in General Sessions Court, Teddy Moss took the witness stand. He explained to the jury how he was an honest businessman preyed upon by Joey, who had tried to take over his thriving check-cashing business.

"Tell us what happened then," asked Assistant DA Kelly.

"I got to the Lunar restaurant about seven," said Teddy. "Joe Gallo comes back to the table and asked Mike what was going to be with this kid . . . 'Do we have to put him in the hospital and give him some time to think, or is he going to be smart and we can be friends and partners and play ball?'"

"Now, as a result of your contacts and conversations with all of these defendants, were you in fear?"

"Yes, I was."

"Were you in fear of physical harm?"

"Yes, I was."

Joey doodled on a scratch pad and stared at the ceiling. Jeffie watched him from the stands. Ignoring Teddy, Joey turned around and smiled. Jeffie didn't have a thing to worry about.

Closing out the witnesses for the Empire State of New York, Assistant DA Clark brought in the NYPD detective, who sat behind Joey's table at the Luna on the evening of the shakedown.

"I can't hear him, Mr. Clark," Joey interrupted.

"What is that?"

"I can't hear him. Tell him to speak louder."

"Will you speak louder, Detective?"

"Yes, sir."

Joey twitched as the detective took the jury through the events of his undercover duty on May 11, from 7:15 PM, the moment he saw Joey enter the Luna, to Teddy's shrimp cocktail.

"They were conversing. Mr. Gallo was overheard to say that . . . Mr. Clark, do you want the language exactly?"

"Yes."

"Mr. Gallo was overheard to say, 'Listen, you fuck, don't talk like a girl. I want straight answers.' . . . Gallo was then heard to say, 'Now listen. You got to come in with us on this deal because I'll put you in the hospital for a couple months, and you'll have something to think about when you are stretched out in the hospital.'"

The jury sat and watched the judge and the good-looking assistant DA and the unimpeachable detective, believing every word, leaving Joey on the outs as a menace to society, a stranger with a big mole, slicked-back hair, and a gangster suit. Staring down the detective as he left the stand and walked past the defense table, Joey shouted, "Motherfucking son of a bitch!" He jumped up to attack before an officer of the court stepped in.

The jury cleared out. Cops surrounded Joey. Looking back at Assistant DA Kelly, the state's righteous golden boy, Joey shouted, "You're a dirty rat. You're framing me," but by then it was all too late. It only took the jury three hours to deliberate.

The People won.

⚊⚌⟪∫⟫⚌⚊

"This defendant has sought to impose the law of the jungle on his victims," said the assistant DA at the sentencing. The state detailed Joey's sorry string of antisocial behavior. Nineteen arrests since the age of eighteen, from vagrancy to attempted sodomy to numerous violations of traffic regulations, not to mention defiance of the McClellan Committee when called to answer for improper activities in the labor field.

"This defendant has firmly made up his mind to pursue a career of violence and crime. His continued predatory role poses a serious menace to decent law-abiding people. He is a determined enemy of society, who has evidenced a complete and utter disregard, even a contempt for duly constituted authority. He has shown no remorse and has given no indication that he would adjust his conduct to the standards of civilized society. For these reasons then, your honor, the People respectfully recommend that no consideration be shown to the defendant on this sentence."

Looking down upon Joey, conservatively dressed in a gray suit and blue tie, the judge imposed the maximum, seven to fourteen years on conspiracy and attempted extortion. A very pregnant Jeffie looked about ready to burst into tears. Joey put his arm around her and said, "Don't worry, don't worry, it'll be all right." The guards put on the shackles. The potato fields rolled by until the rusted spire of Attica appeared on a hill in the middle of nowhere. Guards brought Joey to the gallery in Block B, tossed him in cell number four, and slammed the door shut.

Hype

At his wit's end about how to wipe out the Gallos, protected 24-7 by the best security force in the city, Junior, according to legend, slid a dress on his wild, curly-haired sidekick and sent him off in a red sports car with a trunkload of weapons. The plan was to slip past the Pizza Squad with a wink and a smile, then blast the Dormitory, but somebody tipped off Inspector Martin. He doubled the manpower around President Street, leaving the gunman all dressed up with nowhere to go.

Soon, a fleet of what Inspector Martin called "shotgun riders" roamed through the neighborhood, perfectly legal as the weapons weren't concealed. Cruising along Court Street in a white Oldsmobile, a rider found a sitting duck on the afternoon of December 11, 1961, Gallo man Big Lollypop, coming out of Pintchik's with a can of paint in each hand for the Dormitory. Bullets sprayed from the backseat, hitting Lollypop in the ankle. Paint poured out from a pierced can.

Old Man Profaci was not happy.

The botched Lollypop hit was the latest headline in the

Gallo-Profaci war, a spectacle of vanishing bodies, fish wrapped in clothes, cross-dressing kamikaze raids, and now, drive-bys on paint stores in broad daylight in the middle of one of the most crowded thoroughfares of the borough. According to a Profaci Family informant, there were to be no more attempts on the Gallos unless there were no witnesses, near impossible considering the NYPD encampment on President Street.

Cops made the job tougher upon arresting a shotgun rider on account of the state conservation law, claiming that the loaded weapons endangered the exotic birds and frogs in the Prospect Park Zoo.

Up to his ears in Gallos, Junior exhausted his best tricks by two thirty in the morning on January 5, 1962, as Sammy Davis Jr. wound down his second act at the Copa, heavy with the smell of Chinese food. Junior's beefy dinner companion, Profaci capo Jiggs Forlano, got up from their table at ringside. He walked across the dance floor toward a petite blonde with dark cat's-eye shades, a fur hat, and matching coat, laughing hysterically next to her date, that pudgy, stray Gallo, Sid Slater.

"What the hell are you doing in a fancy nightclub like this," asked Jiggs.

Unaware that Sid was ratting to the DA, Larry had given Sid a bill roll to pay for Jeffie's hospital bill. Sid kept half, three hundred dollars, enough to get a few scotches on the rocks and some champagne. His moll deserved a good night out, having been busy dog-sitting Lepke while Jeffie was in labor.

"Come over to my table," said Jiggs.

Sid headed to ringside. Junior's blood boiled. He wasn't sealed behind an iron fence. He was a tough son of a bitch with real balls. According to varying reports, Sid was grabbed by the tie and given a cheek wound, either by a bite or a "newspaper hook," the kind newspaper vendors use on a ring to open up tabloids.

Captains and waiters in two-toned tuxedo jackets cleared out the area and told the customers to stay away. Blood poured from Sid's nasty wound. He put a handkerchief to his eye and got carted off to the station for questioning. Paparazzi snapped shots of his date, showing off her profile, mugging for the cameras in her big moment.

THAT 'HIT' SHOW AT THE COPA

New York Post
JANUARY 18, 1962

Three in the Gallo gang stood on a barren street corner in black fedoras, hands stuffed into the pockets of their overcoats. A cigarette jutted straight from a lip. Nobody looked at the camera. *Click*. Inside the Longshore Rest Room, a pack of Gallos stood around Kid Blast, who was barking out orders at the table. Big Lollypop leaned on crutches with an ankle cast on his left leg. Weiswasser, the lawyer, put his hand inside his suit coat, looking like he'd pull out a gat instead of another bill. *Click*. Larry stared into the lens in a black porkpie hat. The gang looked their best for the *Life* magazine photographers, posing like real tough guys. The cameras cleared.

Umberto reheated the stale cooking oil and warmed one of the remaining cans of tomatoes on the shelf. Gallos slouched in the freshly painted Dormitory and littered the floor with cigarette butts. Unable to pay Con Ed, they froze in unmade beds with unchanged sheets. Larry brooded as the boys shot stick in purgatory.

Days ran into each other until the afternoon of January 31, 1962.

Smoke poured from the third-story window above Mrs. Gatto's luncheonette down the block.

"Come on!" shouted Larry.

Larry rushed up the stairs. Shrieks of children pierced the heavy black smoke. Punchy grabbed a five-year-old girl with her hair on fire. He snuffed the flames with a couple of whacks of his hand, then snatched a naked baby, wrapped the infant in his jacket and passed him out the door. The Gallo bucket brigade shuttled all six children down the steps and into the thick arms of Mrs. Gatto.

Three fire engines from the 32nd Battalion roared onto President Street, but the fire was out. Larry and Punchy had already tossed the burning mattress out of the window. Back from a trip to buy milk at the grocery store, Sista Biaz, seeing all six of her children safe and sound, dropped her brown bags and wept.

"They save my children," she cried in Spanish. "They are wonderful boys. God bless them."

Kid Blast made the gang empty out their pockets. "We were going to go out soliciting some more," he told reporters, "but then we would have got pinched for extortion." Mrs. Biaz got fifty clams. She hugged the Gallos, posing for pictures in Mrs. Gatto's luncheonette. Blast leaned down to put his arm around her. She kissed him on the cheek. The shutter clicked.

"Don't try to make heroes out of us," Blast told the news cameras. "We're not heroes. We only done what any red-blooded American boys would do. Do you see any horns here? I got no horns. We're not animals. We're just human beings trying to get along."

The tale of the Great Fire went nationwide, picked up as far as the *Seattle Post-Intelligencer*. Fan mail poured into the Dormitory.

A kook from North Carolina wrote:

Hello to the Gallo gang! I read of your act of bravery in saving six children in a fire. That was a great thing for all of you to do. With the good you have in you and the desire to help those in need, surely the fire department, the police department, and your neighborhood need you and they could find something for you to do. I hope to read more and good things about you in the future. The aged, the blind, mothers such as Mrs. Biaz must need young men like you to read to them, to baby-sit, take them for walks. Be brave and ask the police and fire department if there isn't something they can find for you to do.

Admirers from the Midwest sent over a television set so the gang could watch *The Untouchables* on Thursday nights. Housewives baked goods. Militia nuts sent advice on how to best fight guerrilla warfare. The FBI sent dispatches to Hoover, warning, "Considerable favorable publicity concerning the Gallos is expected to result from this action. Subjects should be considered armed and dangerous."

Back at the Longshore Rest Room, the Gallos checked themselves out on the front pages. Big Lollypop poked a pencil through the bullet holes in his fedora and chatted on the pay phone.

"Hey, get off that phone," snapped Punchy. "What if there's another fire? How we going to go put it out?"

"With our crummy luck we'll probably get a ticket for fighting the fire without a license."

"If Joey was here," said Blast, "he would've been the first one up to the fire."

The *Life* feature on the gang war was shelved in lieu of an article entitled "Alright Already, The Mob Is Heroes." Instead of looking like tawdry gangsters, the Gallos graced the pages of America's biggest magazine as saviors of children, replacing the Mercury astronauts as national heroes. The issue hit the newsstands in Miami Beach, the snake- and rat-infested mangrove swamp turned sparkling resort.

Don Carlo Gambino lounged on the sun deck outside Room 218 at the Golden Gate Hotel. He'd been careful not to exert himself, save his trips to the early-bird special at the Rascal House Restaurant, perhaps sneaking the spicy lobster fra diavolo past his wife. No dancing or anything that could get him worked up. The only cloud on the horizon was the trouble of his close colleague, Joe Profaci. Gambino's heart weighed on the strain.

<hr />

Recovered after a bout of smoke poisoning, Larry received a proposition from the big boys. Certain parties in Miami Beach had taken steps to remove Old Man Profaci, rebuild his family, and make Larry a boss, but in order for the plan to proceed,

Larry would have to make peace with Junior. Unthinkable, given Junior's rotten behavior over the past year, but Larry brooded over the Miami Beach proposition in cold logic. A red-blooded American, Larry accepted the dirty realities of big business—the Shanghai wasn't personal—and declared a truce with Junior.

With no army hunting them down, the Gallo gang stepped out of their long winter hibernation. Springtime blossomed in Red Hook. Weeks wore on while the big boys maneuvered, but Larry was patient.

In spite of the truce, Larry refused to leave the security of President Street. He didn't completely trust Junior, and wasn't going to give anyone a second chance at killing him. He enjoyed the company of his father and Kid Blast without worrying about his ulcer. He played violin and looked to the next act.

"I ain't goin' to be doin' what I'm doin' for the rest of my life," he told Inspector Martin, still keeping watch. "You may not think so, but life is made for finer things. One day I'm going to retire. I don't want to be like so many fellows I know who retire and they can't do nothin'. When I retire, I'm going to be cultured. I'm going to sit back and enjoy, enjoy, enjoy."

<hr>

"I got a little pain in my chest," Don Carlo Gambino told a friend on the telephone, but managed to make it back up to New York on March 28, 1962, scooting up the eastern seaboard while situated in car F, drawing room B-52 on the Silver Meteor.

The plastic angel outside the entrance of his quiet old house looked mercifully onto Ocean Parkway in Gravesend,

Brooklyn. A wrought-iron fence wrapped around the tiny front yard. Old Man Gambino amused himself by puttering around the flower garden and pruning his tomato bushes. Small and silver-haired, with a beak nose, he spent every afternoon at Ferrara's in Little Italy, ordering espresso and his favorite pastry. He carefully picked from the fruit stands on Mulberry Street and drove home in the Lincoln Continental to his wife. He owned the Peggy Ann Dress Company in Peckville, Pennsylvania. He seemed like a kindly old man, a ruse honed and perfected over centuries in his native Palermo.

"Joe Profaci has been the father of his family for many glorious years," said Don Carlo, addressing his fellow Dons, "but it is my duty to tell the Commission that for the sake of peace, and to avoid more trouble, perhaps it would be best if he retires."

"It takes a strong and vigorous leader to restore peace," added Don Tomasso, addressing Profaci by his traditional name, Don Piddru. "Why should the serenity of Don Piddru be disturbed? He should be resting, leaving the work to others, to the young."

Don Peppino held his tongue. He had known Profaci since the days of the great feasts at Don Vicenzu's farmhouse, a time to share stories of boyhood in the sun-baked hills of Palermo. Tongues loosened by bottles of wine, the dons would sing odes to loved ones and laments for their mothers. There were bawdy jokes and Sicilian toasts, a test of wit at which Don Peppino was best, composing such rhymes as "Friends, if after this meal I die in Brookulino, I ask to be buried with my mandolino."

"Don Piddru should stay," spoke Peppino, defending his old friend Profaci. He was ready to back up his words with guns, even if it meant waging war against Don Carlo, a "degenerate," as he was known among his peers, for having married his first cousin. "A father has his pride," continued Peppino. "A father doesn't like to leave until he has bequeathed peace to his family." The Commission gave Don Piddru, dying of cancer, full license to do so. Sidge the moneyman shuffled over to President Street to deliver the ultimatum:

If the Gallos commit acts of violence, the Profaci group will immediately retaliate and not only against the Gallos and their men, but against their wives and children.

The Cuckoo's Nest

Taking out his spiral-bound Nifty-Steno notebook, Joey began writing, in pencil, "Nothing is new to me. I have foreseen and am prepared for it all." Mastering a speed-reading technique, Joey devoured six or eight books a day at Attica, shipped in from the Eighth Street Bookshop. He stayed up all night reading philosophy by the dim light that shone through his one small window. "Things exist when I feel they exist, okay?" realized Joey. "Me. I am the world. The world is in me. Good, bad, ugly, beautiful—it's all there. Everything . . . I am alive. I feel it, therefore it exists. And if it exists, it's not good, it's not bad. It just is."

Joey matched wits with Wilde, brooded with Schopenhauer, reasoned with Kant, and was enlightened by Voltaire. He filled his Nifty-Steno with quotes from Nietzsche—"The baits of fools who prefer the company of the unprotesting dead and dare not live dangerously in the perilous future!" He quoted Spinoza on death: "A free man thinks of nothing less than death; and his wisdom is a meditation not of death but of life." He copied out epigrams from eighteenth-century humorist Thomas Hood—"He had to be a lively hood for a livelihood." He devoured books in a heated love affair. "The passion of the intellect," penciled Joey, "which can be as carnal and ecstatic as the rapture of the flesh."

When Jeffie took the eight-hour drive upstate to see him, Joey refused her at the gate, preferring to communicate in passionate love letters. His poetry lifted up to the stars, filled with strange references to an unholy three: the Scorpion's sting, the ice-battering Ram, and the pagan Goat, joining forces with the laugh of a Black Christ. His prose was infused with Arabian Nights imagery steeped in death. Informants gave him two weeks to live.

Larry warned Joey against touching any of the food brought in from the outside. The Profacis had connections behind the walls. They could get him anytime. Tabloids reported a plot to poison the steam table in the mess hall.

For his own protection, Joey decided to get himself "keeplocked," a form of solitary confinement on the block, which meant separation from the general population under close watch. He made a habit of needling the prison guards, the "hacks."

"You have to obey the rules and regulations like everybody else," said the deputy warden.

"I don't believe in obeying rules and regulations," said Joey.

When the keep-lock ended, Joey was thrown out of his cell to mix with the general population. Mafioso were at the top of the heap, leaving Joey to search the Attica yard, Times Square, for backup. The Irish didn't want anything to do with him. Puerto Ricans stuck to themselves. Anybody who wasn't in a gang was a punk. Joey fronted the money for a black nationalist gambling ring, got tight with the brothers, and got a lot of attention from the hacks for breaking the color barrier. They gave it to him good in the shower, where prisoners stood naked in line to get a shot of water, just enough to lather up. The hacks turned up the heat for Joey. He jumped back at the scalding water.

"You know I'm going to win," taunted Joey. "And you know why I'm going to win? Because I've got more *money* than you."

———

The Attica barbershop was a powder keg. Half the barbers were black, half white. Segregated lines led to the prison barber chair, inciting unrest among the black militants. "Half the guys there hadn't been aware that they'd been making a choice about their barber before," remembered Willie Sutton, doing hard time for his infamous bank robberies. "But, boy, all of a sudden the prison was filled with civil libertarians screaming about the sacred barber-client relationship."

To avoid having a civil uprising on their hands, Attica officials ordered one line with a next-open-chair policy, but white prisoners still refused to sit for a black barber, even if his chair was open, especially given the edict of the Klansman in B-block. Standing in the front of the line in the midst of the controversy, Joey waited until a black barber's chair opened up.

The next day in the metal shop, a big guy warned Joey that the Klan was after him. Joey jumped the messenger and got downgraded to punishment detail in A-block, where the Klansman was being keep-locked for reportedly putting a crowbar to an inmate's head. Joey swore the Klansman kept taunting, "I'll get you, Gallo."

Walking down the long, empty hallway on the way to the mess, Joey approached the Klansman's cell and saw a bright red tag hanging outside, indicating that the Klansman was supposed to be keep-locked. He wasn't.

"The guy's screaming," said Joey, telling the story of how he got jumped with a shiv. "The guards think it's me, so nobody shows up for some time. Meanwhile, I'm back in my cell with the door closed and his ear in my mouth. Finally, one of the guards comes, and he hears them talking outside. Then one of them comes in and says, 'Okay, Gallo. Where's the ear?'" In Joey's version, he spit the ear into the toilet and flushed.

Ordered to Reception B for observation, Joey had time to replay the ins and outs of the paranoid B-movie running through his brain. Everybody was out to get him: bounty hunters, Profacis, the Klansmen who threw a burning cross in his cell, the hacks, and in particular, the Nazi, the guard who set Joey up for death by leaving the Klansman's door open instead of keep-locking it—payback for Joey throwing gasoline on the volatile barbershop situation. The prison wanted him dead. And crazy, refusing him any psychiatric care. Nobody was observing him.

Joey felt like an animal in Reception B, less than human, with the same bucket for his waste that was used to clean his tin dinner plate. Sitting in isolation in his six-by-eleven cell, he lived out a hell worse than Sartre had envisioned in *No Exit*. His best chance of survival was a clean slate at a new prison. Joey furnished an appeal to get transferred from Attica on the grounds that his constitutional right against cruel and unusual punishment was being violated by "a deliberate and concerted plan and conspiracy to keep prisoner from inalienable right to select his acquaintances, whether they are white or colored."

The *Post* picked up the story and added the headline, "Trouble Again: Now He's Suing the Warden." The bad press didn't endear Joey to the hacks. He swore that a prison official told him, "You nigger-loving bastard, you'll never live to get the Warden into court." Hardwired against authority, Joey feared he'd snap on a hack, finally giving them reason to beat him to death.

To keep his cool, Joey invented his own sort of primal scream therapy. He lay face down on his cot, buried his face in his pillow, and let out a silent scream at the thought of his enemies while he choked his blanket.

Boned up on the latest from the Eighth Street Bookshop, including rogue psychiatrist R. D. Laing, author of *Sanity, Madness and the Family*, Joey followed the twists and turns of how bouts of psychotic behavior were journeys that led to blindingly clear insight. Super-sane, Joey knew if the guards spying on him through the peephole caught him screaming into his pillow, twisting his blanket, they'd send him off to the nuthouse for sure. Mattawan, the big house of shock therapy, everything detailed in the Village hit *One Flew Over the Cuckoo's Nest*.

After five months under observation without so much as a walk around the yard, Joey turned into a political prisoner, a victim of a conspiracy by the NYPD, the FBI, and the Kennedys, even though Bobby owed him for keeping the mob out of his brother's assassination. In his report to the Warren Commission, the committee investigating the shooting of JFK in Dallas, Sergeant Ralph Salerno listed the ins and outs of the Gallo revolt and concluded, "It is extremely unlikely that the national commission of La Cosa Nostra was involved in any plan to kill the President. It was facing strong internal dissension and other problems and does not appear to have been in a position to undertake such a major act." Joey made everybody on the underworld Commission too crazy to pay any attention to a big conspiracy.

Three days after the Commission gave Joe Profaci the vote of confidence, on Sunday night, April 8, 1962, Joey's old pal, Village boss Tony Bender, got dressed in his nine-room stucco home in Jersey. He affixed the gold cufflinks on his mono-grammed white shirt, slipped on his dark silk mohair suit, and fastened his French wristwatch. Bender took a last look at his wife, Edna, through his horn-rimmed glasses. He said he was going to out buy cigarettes.

"You'd better put on your coat," said Edna. "It's chilly."

"I'm only going to be a few minutes. Besides, I'm wearing my thermal underwear."

Bender stepped out into the night. A squeegee lay on the floor of his new black Cadillac sedan with red interior. After a brutal winter, he'd gotten the garden ready for spring the weekend before. He prepared for summer by cleaning the swimming pool. He had hoped to spend more time in his woodworking shop. He turned on the ignition and drove out onto Palisades Avenue, high on a bluff overlooking the New York City skyline, taking his one-way ride to nowhere. Accord-ing to underworld legend, Tony Bender was in the Cadillac when it got crushed.

As Joey put it, nobody was ever going to put Joey Gallo in a "Tony Bender machine."

Tackling the law library, Joey obsessed over case-law citations and legal journals. With the help of pro bono activist lawyers, drawn to Joey's case on his penchant for civil rights, Joey built his appeal around the enormous amount of press in the months before his trial, much of which he had generated himself.

Jeffie helped him from home by calling *Newsday* on Long Island and asking for clippings, adding them to the *Life* magazine articles, a story in *Time*, Joey's daily headlines in the *Post*, *Daily News*, and *New York Mirror*, and the big feature from that rat Sidney Slater, who had just sold Joey's story to *The Saturday Evening Post* for $20 Gs.

"The amount of publicity given to the defendant rivaled that given to a presidential candidate," his lawyer argued in the petition. "The news media gave so much attention and play to prejudicing the rights of the defendant that legitimate news items, such as the international situation and the atomic bomb, were displaced by headlines concerning the defendant." Joey's appeal rose up the ranks until March 1964, when the U.S. Supreme Court refused to consider it. Searching for any way to buck the system, Joey saw no choice but to go the obvious route.

Arguing for his own insanity, Joey compiled an appeal to prove he was crazy at the time of his trial. He combed through the transcripts for any evidence of mental disturbance and realized his genius. Before getting shipped off to the big house, he had handed the press a handwritten statement deriding the state for forgetting "that there are other Values in our Society which must be balanced against every American Citizen."

Joey quoted Supreme Court Justice Felix Frankfurter, who said, "It is a fair summary of History to say that the safeguards of Liberty have frequently been forged in controversies involving not very nice people."

Joey had yet to realize that liberty didn't come into play when you were Crazy Joe. If he just did his time quietly, he'd be out sooner, but if he stopped fighting, he couldn't win. The lessons of Sun Tzu's *The Art of War* taught him that.

In Mao, Joey learned that all power comes from the barrel of a gun. In Lenin, Joey learned that the revolution must strike twice—there was always a gap between action and total upheaval.

Joey began to write a little black book. Pulling out a new Nifty-Steno, he neatly copied, in ink, a Platonic dialogue between Mao and Lenin, composing a heated debate on revolution.

Lenin: Without a revolutionary theory, there can be no revolutionary movement.

Mao: Knowledge starts with practice, reaches the theoretical plane via practice.

In his own war against the oppressor, Joey struck strong first blows in kidnappings, terrorism against the establishment, and strong displays of force and solidarity, but the real work was yet to come. Comrades were rising up against bourgeois oppressors around the world. The Gallos needed a piece of the action in the global upheaval.

Joey added his own aphorism to his notebook:

Joey: Theory becomes aimless if it is not connected
with revolutionary practice, just as practice gropes in
the dark if its path is not illuminated by revolutionary
theory.

Joey tracked down Willie Sutton in Times Square. The
Revolution could use Slick Willie. The Brooklyn folk hero
stuck up banks during the Great Depression, was an expert
at busting out of prison, and knew how to live underground,
earning him a spot on the FBI Most Wanted List. Joey urged
him to read Mao.

"You get your revolution and what are you going to do
with bank robbers?" asked Willie, chain-smoking rolled-up
Bull Durhams,

"There'd be no banks."

"To hell with your revolution then, Joe."

<hr/>

Jeffie left Attica worried sick. Joey was driving the prison staff
nuts. If he didn't cut out the antics, they'd send him to Mattawan and zap out his brain for good.

"Listen, Larry. He's losing control. He's really going this
time. We got to get him to a psychiatrist."

"If you know somebody and want to send him up, go ahead,
I'll take care of it. But remember. Joey never did a thing in his
life he didn't plan well in advance."

Jeffie sent her shrink, Dr. Bruce, a young Ivy Leaguer and

protégé of her old Reichian therapist, Dr. Albert. Dr. Bruce was led through door after door into the depths of Attica. He ended up in an airless room with a small table, two chairs, and a naked bulb hanging from the high ceiling. It reminded Dr. Bruce of a scene out of Kafka.

A cordon of four guards escorted Joey into the room and locked him in.

Dr. Bruce kept on his game face. Joey was a famous criminal. Dr. Bruce was a professional who could be trusted to give the prison an honest evaluation of Number 62167's mental state. Physically, Joey looked awful, pale and anemic; the prison blues hung on him. Dr. Bruce noted that his eyes looked like burning coals.

Joey took the pad and pencil from the table and scribbled a note:

This room is bugged.

"Doc, you know, I'm glad you brought your instruments with you because I really need a checkup and I don't trust these prison doctors."

The doctor put his stethoscope to Joey's heart. He checked, but couldn't find any bruises.

"You're not going to find any black-and-blue marks," said Joey. He leaned to whisper. "They do it with pillows."

Dr. Bruce held Joey's tongue with a wooden dispenser. Joey brought up Reich's *Mass Psychology of Fascism*, the violence woven into the American fabric, and the "amoral behavior juxtaposed with the Protestant work ethic on which the country was founded."

Dr. Bruce recommended to the prison commissioner that, from a psychological standpoint, Joey's "chances of a more successful accommodation, from both the prisoner's and the authorities' point of view, would be considerably greater at any of the other state prisons than they are at Attica." The commissioner was in full agreement.

The Commission

Only the Almighty had greater pull in South Brooklyn. Every Sunday, Profaci paid Him tribute. The Don gave generously to church charities. In a Bath Beach church, he looked down upon worshippers from the painted ceiling, his face rendered as one of the saints. In another of the local churches, a jeweled crown had been stolen off the Madonna statue, only to be returned by order of Profaci. Word on the street was that the thief got strangled with rosary beads.

The Don had always been religious, but grew closer with the Almighty during his illness. He prayed that his nun sister would help him gain admittance into the Knights of Malta. He ordered a hand-carved replica of St. Peter's Basilica to be installed in his private chapel at Twelve Pines. Some prankster drew nipples on one of the saints.

The Don passed quietly of liver cancer in the late hours of June 6, 1962, at Southside Hospital on Long Island. The funeral was a modest affair with two hundred mourners, duly noted by agents of the FBI and NYPD, who scribbled down the license plates of the limos parked outside at the wake.

After three decades of ruling Brooklyn, the Don was buried in Queens at St. John's Cemetery, entombed in an enormous Romanesque mausoleum in view of the cloister.

"What are you guys so broken up about?" asked Inspector Martin. "From what you told me, he was a heartless, murdering old man."

"Don't talk that way, Mr. Martin," said Larry. "If you can't say something good about the dead, don't say anything."

President Street was in mourning, but Tony Shots didn't shed a tear. It had been almost three years since that cold November evening in 1959 when he had chauffeured his father, Frankie Shots, in the gray Cadillac Imperial to Cardiello's Bar and Grill in Flatbush. Frankie bought a round for everybody. Everybody shook his hand and gave him a hearty sendoff. Two men in topcoats, bandanas, and fedoras blasted him back into the bar. It was a shame. Everybody loved the Bensonhurst numbers man, a nice guy whose only crime was being late on the Don's pizzu.

Packing up his belongings, Tony Shots headed out to President Street. He was a real fighter, big and bald, formerly a fullback at his high school, St. Francis Prep, and part of the 3rd Marine Division at the Battle of Guam. But communal living began to take its toll. Tony started sleeping alone at 49 President Street, one building removed from the rest of the gang. He wore shades to hide the dark circles under his eyes. He had plenty of time to worry about his liver, which he knew he damaged by drinking too much liquor at the Coco Poodle. He downed vitamins.

With the Don dead, justice was served. Tony Shots wasn't sure what came next.

The underworld buzzed how Larry would be next don of

the Profaci Family. After a year of fighting, Larry had earned respect from Bensonhurst to Bath Beach, from the Renaldi brothers to the Bat Boys, from the Sidge to Joe Colombo's boys on Eighty-sixth Street. He made peace with Junior. He deserved an Old World title, but as the weeks passed, the next Don Lorenzo was still the same old Larry, stuck in the same old story on President Street.

Morning after morning, Tony Shots woke up alone, popped his vitamin pills, and put on his shades, leaving him to consider the offer from the Fat Man, Old Man Profaci's brother-in-law. Emissaries promised Tony's widowed mother that all would go well if her son left the Gallos. Otherwise he'd die a nobody like the rest of the outcasts on President Street. She went to the Dormitory to pick up his shotgun. Tony walked out for good and took half of the Gallos with him.

"Who needs him?" growled Larry.

Good and liquored, Larry ordered the last remaining troops to pile into two cars and head for the Copa, hit men be dammed. Yelling at the waiters for more drinks, they banged their fists at the table, rip-roaring drunk. They jumped up shouting, knocking the underside of the round tables with their thighs, sending silverware, plates, and glasses crashing to the floor. The headwaiter told the Gallos to quit making trouble for themselves.

Larry wouldn't listen.

It was his first night out in the real world after a year of being self-imprisoned in the Dormitory. He'd spent all of his time sitting around, smoking cigarettes, and trying to figure out the ins and outs of the brothers' situation, waging motives and considering the power plays, what the Gallos could get away with and what they could not. Joey kept pushing him to act, to let the Gallos off the leash and sic 'em, but Larry held back, hoping he could figure out the answers before taking the Gallos on a death course. He wanted to make good on his promise to the Commission—no violence— knowing one day, he'd be brought before the elders to be approved as don of the Profaci Family. Larry didn't want to answer for broken promises. He didn't want a lot of blood on his hands.

Drinking his fill, Larry hurled insults at all those who'd betrayed him, wishing them damned for eternity, to feel the pain of the iced circle of hell. Larry slunk back into his chair, limp, then staggered up and out of the Copa, leading the rest of the gang back to the Dormitory. The next day, the telephone was disconnected. Weeks later, the electricity was turned off, converting the Gallo funhouse into a dark fortress of broken dreams and loaded shotguns.

<hr>

In his months keeping guard over President Street, Inspector Martin gained no love for the Gallos, but reached a kind of respect. He had never taken up the invitation to share their spaghetti dinners, but now sat at the kitchen table at the dim Dormitory, talking quietly with one of the Gallo boys, "as if we were in a holy place on a sad occasion."

"Why don't you guys go home now?"

"They'll kill us."

"Who will kill you?"

"We're losers. We got beat."

"All right, so you did. Go home. Forget it. Get a job or something."

"That's okay with me. Somebody's got to die, though. You think they'll forget what we done?"

"You could leave town. Start over some other place."

"No. I only know this place. Anyhow, I'm with Larry. I gotta stay."

"Look," a Fat Man emissary told one of the Gallos. "Larry is in bad trouble. He's gotta go. Stay close to him. When you get the word that he's to be hit, you set it up, you hear."

The Gallos were trapped, desperate as the junkyard dogs that howled in Red Hook. There was no more opera on President Street. The illusion was gone for Larry, leaving only the squalor. He had nothing.

He had nothing to lose.

<hr />

Shortly after New Year's 1963, Junior Persico stepped out of his bar on New Utrecht Avenue to his parked Cadillac. He checked around the car to see if anything looked suspicious, then turned on the ignition. Hiding out within eyeshot, the Gallo demolition man flipped the switch to the black box slipped under the hood. "You could feel the explosion right inside your chest," said a witness. "Nobody could have lived through it." The Cadillac launched into the air, then bounced back down on its tires. Junior walked away and brushed himself off.

In another attempt, a Gallo tossed a grenade at one of Junior's bars, but it bounced off a window. The Gallo picked it up to try again. The grenade went off, blowing his hand to shreds. It made him a big hit at the Longshore Rest Room, where he took off his prosthetic hand, put it on the edge of the pool table, set the cue on it, and knocked in the eight ball, this time with dead aim.

Undeterred, the Gallos attached bombs to their remote-control model airplanes and sent them into Junior's turf on a kamikaze raid, but the plan didn't fly.

In the early hours of May 19, a Gallo on a rooftop staked out Junior's latest hideout on Bond Street. Inside a green panel truck, lined with thick fiberglass on the rear and sides and mattresses on the floor to muffle the shots, two Gallos lay in wait with M-1 military rifles, watching through the one-way windows. Shortly before seven in the morning, Junior stepped out into the daylight and slipped into his car, on the move and strapped with his Lugers. The panel truck cut him off on the narrow street. M-1s blasted from the back window.

Bullets shattered the windshield. One bullet hit Junior in the shoulder. Another hit him in the left arm, damaging it for life. According to underworld legend, the bullet continued up his body until it pierced the underside of his cheek and landed in his mouth like a pinball, leaving Junior to spit it out and with his good hand, hand it over to the NYPD detective arriving on the scene. Before the ambulance carted him away, Detective Seedman told the EMS men that he wanted to talk to Junior for a second. Junior's eyes were swollen and blood-caked, though he could still make out Seedman, peering over him and asking, "Who the hell did this to you, Carmine?" Junior spit in Seedman's face. Seedman spit back.

Ali Baba returned to shore after his forty days at sea cooking for the American Export Lines. "I've been everywhere in the world," said Baba. "There's no place like New York!" Profacis shot him down on the Hoboken waterfront.

Baba was revenged three weeks later in Bay Ridge after one of the turncoats who had walked out on President Street, Joe Bats, was shot in his car while waiting for the green light. Profacis revenged Bats by the afternoon, shooting Louie Cadillac in the parking lot of a Long Island shopping mall.

By the day's end, the Gallo-Profaci war toll had reached six wounded, two missing, and twelve dead. Seven had been killed in the past two months, the result of the Fat Man's kill-them-all contract on the Gallos, paid for by skimming a hundred dollars a month from his gambling operations. Brought in for questioning by the Suffolk County DA on the shooting of Louie Cadillac, the Fat Man clutched his chest and acted dazed and confused, then returned to the big house on his East Islip estate.

Installing phone stations throughout the fourteen rooms of his home, the Fat Man kept constant tabs with security to check for any Gallo who might have slipped past the electric fence and the vicious German shepherds. "It was just like *The Godfather*," said Detective Bartels. "Except with big dogs instead of tomato bushes."

Starting the ignition of his car from the kitchen via remote control, the Fat Man braced for an explosion. Hearing none, he walked down the hill to the parked car, a safe distance from the house. The engine purred. The Fat Man sat in the backseat and put the shotgun from the garage across his lap. Even the AC couldn't stave off the heat, all over the Fat Man since a sneaky *Life* cameraman popped a full-page photo of him for that long-delayed cover piece on the gang war entitled "Death Throes of the Gallo Mob":

> They are punks. They are scared. They hide in fear of other hoods and when they do emerge it is with the fright of the hunted animal. Once they were a swaggering gang which killed for hire, assaulted the innocent and dared to rebel against the vicious hierarchy of the U.S. crime syndicate. Now their insurrection has failed, suppressed with equal callousness in a four-year war whose tawdry casualty list has dirtied New York with gangster blood.

But the Gallos didn't fail. They didn't cave. They fought fire with fire in a throwback to the notorious Castellamarese war, a gangland feud to cap the lawless days of Prohibition.

The Fat Man remembered it well.

On one side of the war was the pig Masseria and on the other, the wily Maranzano, so strong he could snap a man's neck between his thumbs. Keeping two pistols and a dagger in his belt, Maranzano dashed through enemy territory and fired a machine gun, swivel-mounted in the backseat of his bulletproof limo. Tabloids printed the lurid tales, quenching the public thirst for blood.

The notoriety brought unwanted attention to the Italian underworld. It was bad for business, and above all, Lucky Luciano was a businessman. Excusing himself to go to the bathroom at a Coney Island restaurant, he left Anastasia to serve the main course to Masseria. Maranzano got it next, killed by

"IRS agents" in his Midtown office who raided with knives instead of a tax lien.

Across the country, the old order was mythically gutted in the second Night of the Sicilian Vespers. When the blood dried, a new order emerged. Capone from Chicago, Magaddino from Buffalo, and from New York City, five who had proven themselves as men of honor: Luciano. Mangano. Lucchese. Bonanno. Profaci. They forged the Commission, bringing order to the underworld until the Gallos came along.

The Commission refused to approve the Fat Man as don of the Profaci Family on the grounds that he could not stop the Gallo war, but the Fat Man knew the truth. Don Carlo Gambino wanted the Profacis at war. He wanted the *Life* magazine articles, the daily headlines, and the six o'clock news. He used the publicity as grounds to oust Profaci and replace him with his errand boy, Tony Bender, thrown to the lions when he no longer served his purpose. Now Don Carlo used the Gallo war as reason to keep the Fat Man from his rightful place as successor to the Profaci Family.

Gambino's lust to rule the Commission had infected the honored ways of tradition, spawned in Palermo that Easter week of 1282, when tax agents from the House of Bourbon handcuffed the faithful on their way to evening prayer. A virgin was raped behind the church. Her mother ran screaming through the dirt-caked streets.

Ma fia, Ma fia!

Rising to serve, a man of honor gutted the filthy Bourbon rapist, an act of defiance that lived on in legend as Night of the Sicilian Vespers. Ready to blast New York City back to the thirteenth century, the Fat Man felt the weight of the shotgun on his belly.

The clock ticked at the Brentwood station of the Long Island Rail Road. Bill Bonanno, son of Don Peppino, sat at the wheel. The train arrived from Penn Station. Sally the Sheik exited and headed for the car.

"Is everything set?" asked the Fat Man from the backseat.

"Yeah, everything's set."

"OK. Start."

⸻

The Fat Man blubbered back when the Gallos took him hostage, but Joe Colombo didn't play the greaseball ruse, feigning weakness to slip out of trouble. A South Brooklyn tough guy raised on movies and jukeboxes, he told the Gallos that if they were going to kill him, kill him like a man. Released unharmed, Colombo didn't hold a grudge, although he didn't appreciate how the Gallos tried to ambush him, lying in wait as he came home from the country club after a round of golf.

Colombo paid less attention to his don than his Dun & Bradstreet rating, rising after a stretch of solid investments on his turf—Kaplan Buick, Cantalupo Realty, and Prospero Funeral Home, solid nest eggs for his sons, Anthony and Joe Jr. Colombo had high hopes for his boys, knowing if an Irish bootlegger could put his sons in the White House, an Italian bookie might be next. He looked ahead to the glass towers of Midtown, where big scores were made with briefcases, not guns, but the Fat Man threatened to drag him back to feudal Sicily.

Waging vendettas against his enemies, the Fat Man expected Colombo to take out Carlo Gambino and his cohorts on the Commission. It was mad, like trying to shoot up IBM.

Colombo played the smart move. He ratted out the Fat Man. Banished for life by the Commission, the Fat Man slunk back to Long Island.

Attorney General Robert Kennedy had been asking for confidential reports to determine the meaning of the Gallo-Profaci war. From his office came a brilliant new strategy to deal with the escalation, a one-line memorandum sent on January 11, 1962, asking, "Why don't we let them shoot each other? Signed, Hopeful."

In the meantime, Kennedy enacted a policy of constant and continual harassment through the Justice Department, cheap shots to whittle away the Gallos on nickel-and-dime offenses. The NYPD arrested the four Gallos more than one hundred times, on charges ranging from vagrancy to consorting to loud and boisterous cards on Umberto.

Not letting up while the going was good, the FBI contacted the Eastern Military Academy, where Larry's son went to school, the tuition paid for with a four hundred dollar check that "disappeared" from the Delmonico Club.

Scouring through Larry Gallo's tax returns, the IRS struck gold upon discovering that Larry obtained a $10,000 G.I. Mortgage from the Veterans Administration to purchase a house in Midwood, Brooklyn. In his application to the Dime Savings Bank to approve the mortgage, a certified letter signed by his father claimed that Larry made two hundred dollars a week in salary at Jackie's Charcolette. Larry's tax returns listed only a fraction of that amount. It was a nothing charge, but the FBI agents told him, "We've got you one way or the other, Larry. You can either admit you were lying on your mortgage application or else tell the IRS that you cheated on your tax return."

Larry wasn't going to go out like Capone. He pled guilty to defrauding the Veterans Administration. In August 1963, backed up by Punchy and four other Gallos sitting behind the guardrail, Larry stood before the judge in Brooklyn Federal Court and took his licks. Four months in jail and fourteen months on probation.

Storming out of court, Gallos pushed newspapermen out of the way as they took Larry down the elevator, leaving behind Umberto in the scuffle. Reporters asked about the $20,000 price on the head of each of his sons.

"They are good boys," said Umberto, "and I think they can take care of themselves."

Shuffling down the seven flights, Umberto prepared to get shipped back to Torre del Greco.

At the start of the gang war, on orders of the Immigration Commissioner in DC, INS officers burst into the headquarters of the Direct Vending Machine Company and arrested Umberto for being an illegal alien. They took him by the arms and dragged him out to the car.

"I'm glad this didn't happen at my mother's house," spat Joey. The old folks on President Street shouted down insults from their fire escapes.

"This man, by his own admission," said an INS official, "entered the U.S. illegally in 1920 by jumping ship in Boston. His file has been open since 1960. There is serious doubt that he can meet that requirement of the law which deals with good moral character."

At the deportation hearing that fall, thirteen witnesses

testified how Umberto worked hard all of his life, from his days engraving at Diagonale & Sons to his current job, sweeping up the floor of the Sidge's factory for fine Italian re-production furniture, two days a week, $1.50 an hour.

Nobody dared say anything against the father of the notorious Gallo brothers.

Now that Umberto was found guilty of defrauding the VA by signing that mortgage letter for Larry, the crime would go a long way toward proving his bad character. The boat to Naples was bound to be bleak, but fate gave Umberto a clear day in Dallas to offset that rainy night on the South Brooklyn piers.

Jack was dead. Bobby left office.

Nobody cared about the Gallos, fading from the limelight after accepting terms for peace and taking their place at the bottom of the newly crowned Colombo Family. Nobody cared about a small-time gang without a good war to read about in the tabloids. Nobody cared to deport an old man like Umberto.

Citizens for Harmony

Joey walked barefoot into the Attica yard, wearing a big straw hat like Van Gogh. He set up his canvas and brushstroked. "Pretty soon," remembered Slick Willie, "there'd be a whole mob of art critics standing around watching him." Transferred out of Attica on the sterling recommendation of Dr. Bruce, Joey branched out into oils. He asked his sister to send him an easel and four canvases on stretchers. His dark and gloomy works ranged from a crouched leopard to a self-portrait, with olive skin against a deep red backdrop and animal eyes. He looked ready to pounce.

Green Haven Correctional Facility was more conducive toward Joey's artistic growth. It was a two-hour drive from Brooklyn, and Joey's family easily made the commute, bringing monthly packages culled from his extensive wish lists, requesting: three cartons of Camels, White Owl cigars, boxes of C. Howard violet mints, Swiss Knight cheese, sour pickles, cans of *bacala*, salmon, and Pastene tuna fish, a head of lettuce, a few pounds of candy, Wildroot hair dressing (New Formula), two dozen "mixed fizzies" (all flavors), and a dozen whole-wheat Syrian loaves from Atlantic Avenue.

Spreading the bread around, Joey doled out gifts to his fellow inmates, expanding his power base across the Green Haven yard, the gang turf of Young Lords, Black Panthers, and Black Muslims, each group congregated in their own section of the yard. Joey roamed free.

"Joey didn't give a shit what you were," remembered Harlem heroin dealer Nicky Barnes. "You'd see him walk around the yard, stopping whenever he'd want and talking to whoever he wanted to."

For the first time in years, not even Profacis had a contract on him, fortunate given Junior Persico's connections in Green Haven. Nicky remembered how Junior's brother Allie Boy stuffed toilet paper into his hat to protect his brain as star quarterback of the prison football team.

"I don't want to play football," said Joey. "What the hell is that shit? Those guys are crazy. You could get killed. I read. I go see the rabbi. I like the rabbi—he's a straight shooter. I don't bother with the priest—a bullshit artist—but I saw a lot of the rabbi."

In the mess, Joey joined a table that relished pulp spy novels. The gangster book club included old-timer Sammy Katz, who first introduced jogging to the yard, chess master Martin Yamin, a former judge turned stick-up man, narcotics wholesaler Matty Madonna, and the black man Madonna groomed to make him rich, Nicky Barnes.

On weekends, the yard opened at noon. Nicky stood in a circle with the Black Muslims, reading *Muhammad Speaks!* They spoke of Lazarus, the need to rise from the grave of irresponsibility and break free from the scourge of the white devils. Nicky spoke about Harold Cruse, who wrote *The Crisis of the Negro Intellectual*.

Joey had finally found a sparring partner to debate finer points of existential philosophy. Talk devolved from Camus to what they knew best. Nicky dug the chicks that came up to visit Joe. "*Beautiful* fucking women," said Nicky, "like they'd just came off of the beach somewhere."

Putting his arm around Nicky, walking him around the yard, Joey laid down the plan through the corner of his mouth.

"He wanted to form a tight-knit cadre to stick up trucks," said Nicky. "Joey loved hijacking."

Joey had his eye on a bigger score, hijacking a Muslim brotherhood. He explained to Nicky how a family was organized, with the don up top and button-men at the bottom. Risk flowed down. Money flowed up. A perfectly oiled machine for pushing heroin, which had been thrown out of whack after the recent Commission dope ban.

Heroin still flowed in bulk from the French Connection to the quiet tenements of uptown's Little Italy in East Harlem, but instead of using their own men to do the dirty work, the ruling class shuffled their packages to black dealers across Lenox Avenue.

Enslaved on a higher plane, a dealer got no stake in the capital. He was kept out of the poppy fields in Turkey, the labs in Marseilles, and the cutting rooms on Pleasant Avenue, where pure dope got weak enough to keep him on a leash, always coming back for more. Harlem was a Wild West of dope, but if the dealers awoke from the Novocain, broke the chains, and got their shit together? Uptown brothers and Gallo brothers could take it to the streets in a truly funky revolution.

⧫

Mayor John Lindsay saw it all melt before him on a scorching July afternoon in 1966. Refusing to have a riot on his hands like the one in Watts the summer before, the liberal, movie-star-handsome mayor went straight to the pressure cooker, the Brooklyn neighborhood of East New York. Without sending his advance men to check out the hostile territory, Lindsay toured the south side of New Lots Avenue, predominantly Italian working class.

"Go back to Africa, Lindsay, and take your niggers with you!" a resident shouted.

The mayor entered Frank's Restaurant on New Lots Avenue, situated on the racial dividing line. He told the customers that they should talk together and try to work things out.

Gathering outside on a triangular concrete traffic island, forty white youths from SPONGE, the Society for the Prevention of Negroes Getting Everything, picketed the mayor, chanting, "Two, four, six, eight, we don't want to integrate!" Police barricades rose. Forty young black men who wanted their face time with the mayor marched in from the north side of New Lots, but a patrol car had already shuttled Lindsay back to Manhattan. SPONGE picketers crashed through the barricade.

Shots rang out. A sniper fired from a rooftop, killing eleven-year-old Eric Dean. Hundreds arrived at the scene.

United Black People circulated leaflets to the crowd, which informed, "Whitey has done it again—innocent Eric Dean was shot down by white racist cops or gangs—Whitey wanted for murder, justice now."

Gangs ran through the Italian section of New Lots in search of "Whitey." Molotov cocktails dropped from the rooftop of an apartment building. Three hundred policemen arrived at the scene. Dr. Frank C. Arricale, the City Youth Board director, learned that gangs of Italians and blacks prepared to converge on New Lots to shoot it out. In the heyday of juvenile delinquency, the 1950s, Youth Boarders would hang around the candy stores and dole out smokes to get an in with the gangs. Acting as missionaries rather than beat cops, members of the controversial organization did anything in their power to curb gang violence, even sitting on war council meetings, trying to get rivals to agree to a fair one. Now, even the all-out Prospect Park rumble of the South Brooklyn Boys seemed tame compared to what lay ahead. Accompanied by Youth Board adviser Rabbi Schrage, founder of the Maccabees, a vigilante group roaming the streets of Crown Heights, Dr. Arricale headed out to President Street. Pete the Greek stood on guard on the corner.

"It was a rabbi, alright," said the Greek, "a real Jewish rabbi, complete with the beard, yarmulke, and all."

Rabbi Schrage told the Greek that he was looking for the Gallos. The sit-down occurred at Roy Roy's Luncheonette, a few doors from the Dormitory. Kid Blast sent off the gang and offered his guests cigarettes. He introduced Rabbi Schrage to his father.

"You do it," said Umberto.

Blast sat with his lawyer, Dr. Arricale, and Rabbi Schrage

over sodas and smokes. He wanted to know how the Youth Board proposed to keep the kids off the streets. "If you stop the fighting," said Blast, "it'll happen again next week. What are you going to do for an encore? What about education and jobs? They have no preparation. What are you do-gooders going to do about that?" Larry and Joey hoped Blast would be the one to go to college. Blast was bitter about having to educate himself on President Street. He wanted to know what was in it for him.

"The Rockefellers started out as a bunch of robber barons, but by doing good works their name is blessed," said Dr. Arricale. "Maybe the Gallos could do the same thing."

"From your lips to God's ear," said Blast, flashing a grin to Rabbi Schrage. He agreed to help. The rabbi promised to pray for the Gallos, but stressed that the nature of his job should be on "social work," not strong-arming.

Armed with a signed letter identifying him as chairman of the Emergency Citizens for Harmony in East New York, deeming him "an ad hoc intergroup relations committee working to ease community tensions," Blast made his way to New Lots Avenue.

Meeting with the Italian gang leaders at a local restaurant, Blast stood at the head of a long table and announced, "The purpose of this meeting is to avert bloodshed. I expect you to feel the way I do. Anyone who doesn't, say so right now, and I'll pay for his psychiatric fees. I'm not here to listen to your problems or your grievances, and I know they are many. Tell the rabbi about them later. But it's too dangerous to take the time now. How are we going to stop people from killing? Any suggestions?"

"*We're* not looking for trouble," said one angry youth. "It's the others."

"Then what are you doing in East New York? Shut up and sit down."

—◦◦◦◦◦◦—

"I hear a rumor the Gallos have been asked to make peace in New York," said Elliott Golden, the chief assistant to Aaron E. Koota, Brooklyn DA.

"That's incredible," said DA Koota.

The Gallos were the bane of public decency, an affront to law and order, and a waste of taxpayer dollars. On January 8, 1965, Judge Renaldi of the State Supreme Court sentenced Larry and Blast to six months on assault. He slapped six months on Punchy, three months on ten other Gallos, fines. DA Koota hailed it as a "milestone in the history of criminal prosecutions in New York." He only wished the judge could throw the key into the Gowanus.

Koota demanded that the Gallos meet him at his office in Borough Hall, but the brothers refused to show. "They have nothing to gain from such a meeting except further notoriety," said their uncle, Joseph Iovine, Esq. Uncle Joe told the press that the Gallos were happy to assist the civic community and would like to develop a "new image" of themselves as servants to law-abiding citizens over racketeers.

"You can't always deal with people who are leaders in the Boy Scout movement," concluded Mayor Lindsay. "Sometimes you must call upon individuals with fairly rough backgrounds. I, as Mayor, don't live in a cocoon. It was hot and dangerous at the time, and I am very thankful that all aspects of the neighborhood agreed to cool it."

The Mayor said he would "certainly" call on the Gallos again if the need arose.

—◅ⅧℯⅧ▻—

White guards stood on the prison catwalks with rifles, ready to shoot down inmates like rabid dogs. Oppressed by Gestapo tactics of strip searches and beatings, the prisoners spoke out against the cruel and unusual punishments of the imperialists. The time had come to break down the walls separating Black Muslims, Black Panthers, and Five Percenters. It was time to unite all of the prison's four hundred black nationalists, a fourth of the population in the concentration camp called Auburn Correctional Facility.

On November 2, 1970, honored as Black Solidarity Day, inmates refused to grind out industrial products in boiling slave-labor sweatshops, which contributed nothing to the pockets of the people, but to the free-enterprising connections of the racist Empire State.

For five hours, the strikers sat around the yard, played ball, and returned peacefully to their cells while the fourteen strike organizers were keep-locked. Two days later, the Black Solidarity Day Movement told the yard not to line up for work detail until the superintendent returned the keep-locked strike organizers to the population. Raising their voices over the PA system, on a platform in the middle of the central yard, the Black Solidarity Day Movement leaders announced that their fourteen keep-locked brothers must be released. Fists went up in the air. No more shucking and jiving. Fists went up in the air. They were going to get what they wanted or die trying. Fists went up in the air.

This wasn't just for black militants, but Young Lords, denied Spanish-speaking guards to listen to their needs. It was even for Whitey.

The Black Solidarity Day Movement rallied whites across the yard to join. Inmate number 62167 was invited to give a speech to rally the cause. If he didn't take a stand on the platform, he was part of the disease. Taking the mike, Jocy told the whites to stay out of the "black thing." The crowd booed and cursed him as the white devil. A prison sergeant forced his way up on the stand to regain control, but no use. The Black Solidarity Day Movement put the heat on the crowd.

The word was out. The inmates were going to take over the prison. They outnumbered the guards twenty-five to one. Hostages would be taken.

Joey forced his way back onto the podium. He told the whites to cool it. If there was a riot, wait it out in a corner of the yard. If an officer ordered them back to their cells, do it. He said he'd die if he had to, but nobody was going to stop him from following the orders of the hacks. The crowd got angry.

"All hell broke loose," said one witness.

Grabbing clubs from the guards and lengths of pipe, revolutionaries secured Auburn's four cellblocks. Fueled by shouts breaking through the PA system, railing against the fascist regime, comrades cut off the prison telephone service, herded up white guards, dragged them to the center of the yard, poured on gasoline and threatened to light up. Joey ran to get a knife from "the Polack" in A-block.

Pushing through the rioters, Joey made his way to a

hostage, a prison guard injured in the siege. Joey dragged him out of danger, down to the lower hall for medical treatment. No one tried to stop Crazy Joe. Word in the joint was that he could bite your ear off.

As the siege raged in Auburn, prisoners insisted on a meeting with Governor Rockefeller.

"They want the works," reported the commissioner.

Better clothing, a revision of the rules on censored letters, more black social programs, a competent psychiatric staff, additional Parole Board hearings, Spanish-speaking guards, healthier food, an expanded law library, and the release of all fourteen keep-locked brothers.

Two hundred state police got ready to smash through the gray-brown walls of Auburn to demonstrate what happened to rebels.

"Cooler heads prevailed," said the deputy superintendent. The revolt was over by that evening as seventy-two revolutionaries were cordoned off into special disciplinary areas. They threw shit on the guards in protest. One claimed that a guard went at him with an axe handle while another said they used a fire hose. A group from the Youth Against War and Fascism took the bus up from Manhattan, demanding the release of the "Auburn Six, the Auburn 72, and all political prisoners."

In his gray-roofed colonial in Merrick, Long Island, Larry opened the refrigerator, kept stocked by his wife on her daily trips to the supermarket. Dropping several ice cubes in his glass, he added Scotch to his milk to make a brown cow, his signature drink. His youthful feats of daring on President Street long forgotten, Larry's notoriety now rested as the local mobster. Once Larry's son let the family dog go on the neighbor's yard.

"I told my wife to tell him to cut it out," said the neighbor, "then I found out who he was and I told her not to say anything."

Putting Verdi on the hi-fi, Larry let himself out onto the back deck, looking out over South Oyster Bay. With no hit men lurking in the suburban streets with a trunkload of shotguns and grenades, Larry had time to reminisce on his golden years of running numbers for Frankie Shots, and on Larry, Joey, and Kid Blast, the mob prodigies who were destined to become the next Murder, Inc. Larry sipped his brown cow, enjoying prestige, respect, and peace as a capo of the Colombo Family.

"For a while it looked as though Larry would make it," remembered Pete the Greek. "But he wasn't making anything. He was dying hard and he knew he was dying."

In late 1967, Larry began a cobalt treatment for cancer. His operation at St. Vincent's left him shriveled in his bed, propped upright, shivering in a fever under a hospital blanket.

"Where's Joey?"

"He's coming," said the Greek. Joey had arranged for a leave to see his dying brother.

"He said he'd come and he'll come."

When Joey strode into the hospital room, Larry looked off, like he hadn't been waiting for years.

"What're you shaking for?" asked Joey.

Larry said it was the bed.

Joey told him to get his old lady in the sack with him, like Jane Russell in *The Outlaw*, to keep warm.

At Joe Colombo's Prospero Funeral Home on Eighty-sixth Street in Flatbush, FBI men clicked their mini-cameras across the tree-lined street from St. Rose of Lima's, a gray limestone church. Twenty-seven limos pulled up. Seven pallbearers carried Larry down the steps. Five cars driving slowly, covered in flowers, led the wreathed procession into Green-Wood Cemetery. The chrysanthemum-laden mahogany coffin was lowered into the open grave.

<hr />

When the crowd at Auburn strained to hear what Joey was going to deliver though the mike, he could've sparked them on, hell-bent on a bloodbath, like the one to take place a year later at Attica. But up there, in front of the yard, Joey had a moment of clarity. Why should he die for the Revolution? The black nationalists called Joey a Judas for betraying their cause, but the superintendent wrote him a memo praising his "commendable acts" in the heat of the riot. As a reward to Prisoner Number 62167, the commissioner approved Joseph Gallo's Good Behavior Allowance Report. Five years of "lost time" for rotten behavior were regained. Joey was sent to Sing Sing to finish out his last months, safe from the death threats of the Black Solidarity Movement. He turned forty-two on April 6, 1971.

For the first time in his life, Joey took the sacraments, from someone he had once called a bullshit artist, a prison chaplain affiliated with Lincoln Hall, a Catholic institution for juvenile delinquents. Joey told his parole officer that he planned to speak to the boys on leading productive lives and "finding employment," despite never holding a steady job himself.

The Stampede

Nobody disrespected Joe Colombo on his turf, Cantalupo Realty, sitting on a stretch of Eighty-sixth Street in Bensonhurst. "He has the sincerest group of clients," said Anthony Cantalupo. "They don't cheat him out of his commissions." Aside from his real-estate interests, Colombo earned thirty dollars off of every car sold at Kaplan Buick across the street. The glossy showroom was a perfect spot to conduct family business. If a cop tried to break up a meet, all a guy had to say was, "Hey, buddy, I'm just looking to buy the wife a Buick." Customers were thorough, sometimes stopping by for weeks before they broke down and signed the papers to finance a Skylark. Buicks became the new Cadillac in the Colombo Family.

A respectable car salesman, Colombo didn't like how an ever-present FBI agent, a big Irishman named Bernie Welsh, stood on the sidewalk in front of Kaplan Buick and howled, "Whoo! Joe!" To remedy the problem, Colombo goons led Denis Dillon, head of the Federal Strike Force Against Organized Crime, by the arm into Cantalupo Realty. "Don't worry, Mr. Dillon," said Colombo, "nothing's gonna happen to you. But these agents, they don't respect me."

"The federal men are lousy," Colombo griped to Detective Seedman of the NYPD. "They are bigots. I expect they will be after me before long. I'd never say this to my family, but I swear to God the FBI is going to frame me somehow."

On April 30, 1970, the FBI booked Colombo's pride and joy, his fat twenty-three-year-old son, Joe Junior, on conspiracy to melt silver coins into ingots. That very evening, Colombo got Sammy the Bull, Shorty Spero, and a handful of the family's heavy hitters to picket the FBI's Upper East Side headquarters on Sixty-ninth Street and Third Avenue. They sounded like the Seven Dwarfs. "Hi de hi de hi de ho, FBI has got to go! Hi de hi de hi de ho, FBI has got to go!"

Shuttle buses ran to pick up wise guys from their Brooklyn social clubs, dropping them off to join the evening picket. They'd settled into a routine—shout for an hour, then travel up two blocks to P. J. Bernstein's for corned beef. It made surveillance easy for the Feds. Taking pictures of the picket line, they got a complete portfolio of the Colombo Family, whose boss wore a wide, striped power tie and took to the airwaves like he was running for the Senate. "I'd see Colombo on the late news with that overweight son of his beside him," said Chief Seedman. "They'd claim the Mafia was a myth, that we law enforcement officials were pinning all the ills of society on Italian-Americans."

On *The Dick Cavett Show*, Colombo said he was just an average guy who owned a piece of a funeral parlor. The audience snickered. Colombo didn't think it was funny. The audience clammed up.

Believing that he was ordained to do "God's work," Colombo put the heat on Alka-Seltzer's "Spicy Meatballs" commercial, which depicted a round Italian woman, her hair in a bun, serving up a mound of spaghetti and meatballs. "Mamma Mia," cried her suspendered, mustachioed husband, "datsa spicy meatball!" Programmers pulled it.

Headquartered in a sleek skyscraper office on Madison Avenue and Fifty-ninth Street, staffed by men in pastel ribbed turtlenecks, Colombo's Italian American Civil Rights League took on the politicians. An honorary League member, Governor Nelson Rockefeller ordered New York State law enforcement to cease using the terms Mafia and Cosa Nostra. Attorney General John Mitchell issued a similar order to the Justice Department.

The politicians caved easily, leaving Colombo to take on Hollywood big shot Al Ruddy, who was in the midst of producing the film version of Mario Puzo's *The Godfather*. An epic depicting the three Corleone brothers battling the Five Families of the New York City underworld, Puzo's bestselling novel had the makings of a blockbuster, but angry locals and threats of union walkouts plagued location shooting in East Harlem and Little Italy.

To fix the problem, a sit-down was arranged between Al Ruddy and fifteen hundred League delegates, some booing, in the Grand Ballroom of the Park Sheraton Hotel on February 25, 1971. Insisting his film wasn't about negative *mafioso* stereotypes, but poor immigrants faced with prejudice, Ruddy explained that the bad guys weren't even all Italian. Take Captain McCluskey, the crooked Irish cop, or Sollozzo, the wily Turk who was good with a knife.

"How about a good kid from Bensonhurst?" asked Colombo.

Ruddy got the picture. Colombo picked *Godfather* extras from the cheering crowd.

Shuttling between the sidewalk of FBI headquarters, Madison Avenue, and Cantalupo Realty, Colombo prepared to do God's work on the next man who dared defame him, this time no pushover from Washington or Hollywood, but Crazy Joe Gallo.

Alarms sounded across South Brooklyn, warning of Crazy Joe's imminent return from the joint. "He'd break up a High Mass if he felt like it," said a detective on the Pizza Squad. "Inside of a week, that guy could destroy everything that had been done over a couple of years." The running joke in the Colombo Family was that Joey was going to start making "black buttons" in the Gallo gang, using his black nationalist prison connections to build an army of number-runners and heroin-pushers in the largely black neighborhood of Bed-Stuy.

Nobody knew what Crazy Joe was capable of, not even Kid Blast, who drove out to Sing Sing to pick up his older brother, savoring his last moments as the acting head of the Gallo gang. Following Blast on backup, with an itchy trigger finger, was Bobby Boriello of the bell-bottomed Boriello brothers. During the Gallo-Profaci war, Bobby stood on a milk crate as a lookout on President Street. "A kid that could break your heart," said Detective Bartels. Now a husky teenager, Bobby led the Mod Squad, a pack of pot-smoking wild boys, ready to raise hell at the release of Crazy Joe, the living legend of Red Hook.

In the kitchen of her Fourth Avenue rooming house in Flatbush, Mary prepared for her Joey.

"Put some weight on him, Mama," said Pete the Greek. "He needs it. Give him lots of pasta."

Up in the attic, Jeffie picked out the right lingerie in front of the mirror, something sexy and funky to accompany Sly and the Family Stone on the turntable. She wanted everything to be just right after living on Joey's letters. Her daughter, Joie, had only known her father as a prisoner.

A crowd waited on Mary's porch. Hundreds lined up to touch Joey's face and hold his hand. NYPD prowlers jammed the block, ready for Blast to pull up with the hood. Joey emerged thin and pale. As she had ten years before in Manhattan Sessions Court, when she kissed his manacled hands, Mary wept.

"All right," said Joey. "I'm home. Let's cut out the bullshit crying. Just show me what's there to eat."

Joey sat at the table, performing for visitor after visitor, wisecracking like the good old days. His mother served round the clock, cooking, muttering under her breath as she stirred the sauce.

"Listen, baby," asked Jeffie, "why don't you cool it? She's an old lady. She's tired."

"Oh, she loves it," said Joey.

Al Lettieri, the square-jawed Sicilian who had left the San Remo years ago to become an artist, stopped by with a bottle of Dom. In town for *The Godfather*, he was playing a role he could finally sink his teeth into, Sollozzo the Turk, the tough narcotics dealer. Jean showed too, that nutty cat girl who on a snowy night told Joey, over a bottle of brandy in a Village dive, that he needed to paint, write, sing, dance. She hadn't given up.

"You must write a book while it's fresh on your mind!" she insisted.

Jean told him that his book needed to be serious, drawing from his vast reading in prison, his letters and poetry, his ideas on art and his philosophies of life. Nothing cheap, nothing sensational, nothing having to do with crime.

"Yeah," said Joey. "Yeah, I'll do it, I'll do it."

He told his parole officer that he was thinking about a play based on his prison years, something like Jean Genet's dark tales of prison, where beauty grew from the underbelly. He could get across an important statement, conveying his strong belief that most inmates were mentally ill patients who needed to be under psychiatric care. Something like the hit play *Marat/Sade*, set in an asylum, exposing the system's hypocrisy.

Determined to settle down and write, Joey moved into an eighth-floor, fully carpeted apartment in a doorman building on West Fourteenth Street in Union Square, just north of the Village. He took long walks to catch up on the life he'd missed, digging the fruits of women's lib, the braless chicks in Washington Square Park.

"Greek, Greek," he said, jabbing his bodyguard. "Look at *that* one. Mamma mia. Look at those boobies bouncing."

Joey took his daughter to see the violent and bloody *Bonnie and Clyde*, playing at the St. Mark's Cinema. He walked past the remains of the townhouse on West Eleventh Street that had been accidentally blown up by the Weathermen, a revolutionary cadre of spoiled blue bloods who couldn't even wire a bomb.

"It was all different," said the Greek, "like his fucking pants were different. I'd ask him when he was going to get with it. He'd say, 'Don't give me none of that jive talk, Greek.'"

On Fourteenth Street, Joey ran into Detective Bartels'

son, a good-looking kid who worked as a sales clerk at Barney's men's department on Madison Avenue. "Barney's?" asked Joey with a smile, furling his fingers into a fist, wondering if the kid would pick up on the gesture. Did he want to lift some swag? The kid declined.

Jeffie updated Joey with a collection of chic menswear. Joey gave it all away to the Mod Squad. He thought the groovy shirts were for fags and hated how the pants weren't pleated, leaving no place to put his balls. He settled on a leather jacket, a peaked felt cap, and toned-down bell-bottoms, but wouldn't budge on his music.

Jeffie hit up Umberto for one hundred dollars to buy all the great records Joey missed out on, *Blonde on Blonde*, *The White Album*, *Let It Bleed*. Joey wanted Bing Crosby and Miles Davis. He hated Jeffie's records, especially *Chestnut Mare* by the Byrds, co-written with Jacques Levy. The title song was about a wild horse, free from the reigns that shackled men to a desk and a dental plan.

"I don't want to hear any fags singing about any fucking horse," snapped Joey.

"It's not about a fucking horse," said Jeffie. "If you'll listen, it's about life."

Jeffie put it on while Joey was in the tub, hoping it would relax him. Sopping wet and naked, he grabbed the record off the player and tossed it down the incinerator in the hall. Joey had a hard time easing into the seventies, unlike his little brother, Blast, whose mutton chops and big Elvis shades made him look like the next James Taylor. Blast took it easy while Joey was away. For Colombo's birthday, Blast got the Gallos to park a truck on Eighty-sixth Street and wheel out a new golf cart. The Don was a big shot at the public golf course in Dyker Park.

Returning the favor at Christmas, Colombo handed out ties on President Street. Everybody got the same one. Even Agent Welsh gave Blast the upraised brow.

"You get him a golf cart, and he gives you *ties*?"

Blast played it cool. He was too cautious to go shoot up the boss, despite Colombo having failed his promise to "spread the bread around." This distracted Joey to no end, just as he was settling down to write.

"Had that cocksucker good," seethed Joey, remembering the days when he had held Colombo hostage. "Had him in my hands. Should have killed him then. Just knew I should have killed him."

The only love Joey had gotten from Colombo was an envelope holding $1,000 in cash to help fund his welcome back dinner. No personal visit, no overdue concessions from the Gallo–Profaci settlement. Not a penny of the millions Colombo made off his Italian-American Civil Rights League.

At the Feast of San Gennaro on Mulberry Street, the League sold "Numero Uno" buttons for ten dollars and Italian flag buttons for five. Sinatra's concert at the Felt Forum raised half a million for the League. Thousands sent ten-dollar dues to the head office. Burly League reps canvassed the luncheonettes and pizza parlors of South Brooklyn for heartfelt "donations."

Joey could handle getting squeezed out of the action. That was what happened to Gallos. But when Colombo sent his capos, Rocco Miraglia and Gallo turncoat Nick Bianco,

in a gold Buick station wagon to President Street, to demand
that Joey put up posters for their upcoming Unity Day rally?
On Gallo turf?

"Grease the pistols," Joey told the Mod Squad. "The move
is on."

Joey tore up the posters, kicked the capos off President
Street, and told them that the only reason he let them live was
to deliver a message to that "fucking queer" Colombo: no
League paraphernalia on Gallo territory. Hell-bent on destroy-
ing the League, Joey, the former revolutionary turned anti-civil
rights reactionary, waged a counterrevolutionary propaganda
blitzkrieg.

Taking the offensive, Gallos ripped off Unity Day posters
hanging along Court Street and announced to Red Hook that
the only interests the League represented were Colombo's
own. Business owners were ordered to keep their shops open
during the rally and not to insult the Italian people by letting
employees go.

"Usually store owners felt they were caught in the middle,"
said the Greek, "that if they didn't attend, Colombo's people
would come down on them, and if they did, we would. The answer was simple. We were a lot closer than the Colombos."

Stoned and psyched to go to the mattresses, the Mod
Squad barricaded President Street. They played slapball on
the block and dug out a huge outdoor pool in a vacant lot
across from the Longshore Rest Room. The gang mixed concrete, trying hard not to get it on their fine Italian loafers, but
didn't pour it level, leaving the surface lopsided. Neighborhood kids splashed around in the day. At night, the grill in the
Hawaiian gazebo sizzled. The chippies came, romanced pool-
side under the starry skies of Red Hook.

On dog days, bell-bottomed Bobby Boriello chunked cantaloupes down President Street and aimed the fire hose at Mondo the Midget, shooting him off the ground and up the brick wall. Stuffing a huge can full of fireworks, Bobby set it in the middle of the street and lit it up. Bottle rockets and cherry bombs blasted and shot all over the block.

Like old times, Umberto was happy again to cook big pots of spaghetti, excited at the prospect of being a big shot now that his sons were taking on Colombo. He tipped off FBI Agent Welsh on a secret of good cooking: always put oranges in the salad. Welsh became a fixture on President Street, sitting around and eating with the boys, figuring that if he got on good terms with them, he might be able to turn one as an informant. Joey told him to forget it. No one was squealing for nobody, but Joey said he appreciated how nice Welsh had been to his mother.

Closely observing, Welsh thought Joey was a character, a little like Tommy Udo, a lot like Frank Gorshin, the twitchy comedian who played the Riddler in the campy television series *Batman*, the Gallos' favorite show. A trickster at heart, Joey claimed to have something up his sleeve for Colombo's upcoming Unity Day. Nobody knew what, but shortly before the big rally, Joey pulled aside Agent Welsh and asked, concerned, "Bernie, you're not gonna be out there that day, are you?" He was. "Then be careful. I hear there's gonna be a *stampede* that day."

⚊⚋⚌⚍⚎⚏

Colombo stepped out of his chauffeured Buick at Columbus Circle. He unbuttoned his white, short-sleeved shirt at the col-

lar. An electric organ ground out a melody. Plastic streamers
in red, white, and green stretched from the Columbus statue
to the lampposts around the southwest corner of Central Park.
Two hundred and fifty thousand people were expected to turn
out for the Second Annual Unity Day. Thousands had already arrived early. Old men in plastic straw hats waved
miniature Italian flags. Girls in hot pants with "Kiss Me, I'm
Italian" buttons gave the upraised index finger of Italian
Power.

Plainclothes detectives scanned the crowd for trouble.
Colombo told the NYPD he didn't want a lot of uniformed
cops. He wanted to keep it festive. Colombo Family bodyguards stuck guns under their summer shirts although it was
hard to miss the bulges.

Colombo took a look at the day's schedule resting by the
speaker's stand, covered in red, white, and blue bunting. Mr.
America was going to flex.

Dozens of photographers surrounded Colombo. A young,
lanky black man in a polo shirt bobbed toward him, thirty feet
away, with a Bolex movie camera. He wore a big watch and
gold rings.

"Watch him," directed Colombo.

The movie bug infected this young man, Jerome Johnson.
He had left his home in New Brunswick for a stint in Hollywood. He wanted to be a filmmaker. As he drifted along the
Sunset Strip, his good looks and reefer connections turned him
on to the right people and hippie chicks willing to take him into
their bungalows. He seduced them with astrology pickup lines
and a book of poetry, which he showed the LAPD when they
picked him up early one morning, wandering outside the
palaces of Beverly Hills. He said he was visiting a woman. She'd

given him the book as a gift. The cops told him never to step foot in the Hills again.

After two years in California, Jerome returned home to New Brunswick, where he cruised the Rutgers campus in the backseat of a rented Cadillac limo with a chauffeur. A smooth operator, he gave coeds at the student union his business card, Johnson Productions, Inc. One two-hundred-pound blonde put him up for a bit, claiming, "He was the best lover I ever had, on a technical basis. He was hung like an elephant."

After spreading his seed at Rutgers, Johnson found himself around Harvard, in the summer of 1971. A wooden scimitar dangling from his belt, he leaned down to a redhead reading under a tree and said, "I'm a male witch. Can I tell your fortune?" She took him to her commune. He hung around for a few days, smoked reefer, and talked films. He'd been an extra in a Village art film directed by Hauser. The commune got tired of listening to Johnson go on and on. He split to Canada, where a hospital administrator picked him up on a wooded road in Medicine Hat.

Johnson talked about his production company and the ins and outs of making films in New York, Hollywood, and Canada. Swinging down to Philly, he crashed at the pad of his man Van Kirksey, a black actor who had roles in *Uptight* and *Cotton Comes to Harlem*.

On Sunday evening, June 27, Johnson took a bus up to Port Authority in Manhattan. He lived on and off with a Slavic girl on Christopher Street, but kept his things in a spare room in the Perfumed Gardens, a massage parlor in the Chelsea Hotel, and a bare studio on Elizabeth Street. That was where he kept his trunk. Inside were a few feathers, an astrology book, an incense box, and a picture of him dressed up like a cowboy. Rather than go to his studio, he decided to stay with a friend of his, a black actress who lived in the Village. He showed up at her door with a yellowish spider monkey he kept in a cage. She was busy rehearsing a role. Johnson asked if she wanted to have dinner. She already had plans. Johnson said that was fine with him. "I got work to do anyway. Got to get myself together for an important job tomorrow."

"Doing what?"

"I'm going to shoot Colombo."

On June 28, the morning of the rally, Johnson showed his League press card to security, allowing him access into the inner circle around the Columbus statue. With him was his assistant, whom the police later identified as either a woman or a man in drag. She had a midsize Afro and great curves, which she showed off in tight clothes, from varying accounts either blue jeans, slacks, or a miniskirt. Colombo's bodyguards checked her out. A powder horn dangled from her hip. She packed a black German Menta automatic made in World War I.

Fifteen feet from Colombo, Johnson crouched down to get a good shot. The gears of his Bolex movie camera turned.

"Hi, Mr. Colombo," said the girl. She smiled.

Johnson kept the Bolex to his eye as he unloaded three bullets into Colombo's head.

"They got Joe!"

A pile jumped on top of Johnson. Somebody fired three shots into Johnson's back, killing him instantly, and walked away clean. The camera assistant slipped past the cops. Colombo's bodyguards raged through the crowd, attacking blacks at random. A gang of six jumped on a guy with a Mohawk and two axe handles under his belt, a guitar player who was to perform that day.

"Kill him!" screamed the onlookers. An ambulance rushed off Colombo.

A spokesman for BRAT, the Black Revolutionary Attack Team, called the Associated Press, claiming, "We have just assassinated Joe Colombo. It is only the beginning. White people will continue to pay for their crimes against black people." Joe's son Anthony called a press conference, denying any conspiracy.

"It was the act of one maniac acting alone. This is what they do now to all civil rights leaders."

Outside Roosevelt Hospital, where Colombo lay in a coma, FBI agents searched his bodyguard, Vinny Vingo.

"I hope you're doing this to the Gallos too," snapped Vingo, "because they shot Joe Colombo."

<hr>

"Colombo comes out of his coma. He asks for something to drink and sees the bottle of wine at his bedside, made by Ernest & Julio, the Gallo brothers. Colombo goes right back into a coma again."

Crazy Joe giggled at his own joke, telling it to anyone who'd listen. He rolled his crazy Riddler eyes when Agent Welsh pulled him aside for a chat.

"My God," said Welsh, "that's unbelievable. How do you think you're gonna get away?"

To have a black man shoot Colombo was like Joey leaving a "calling card," as former *New York Times* reporter Nicholas

Gage put it. The *Daily News* splashed a picture of Joey alongside Jerome Johnson with the caption, "Befriended Blacks in
Prison." Joey said Colombo had it coming for making himself
a celebrity, a ready-made target for any "crazed nut," but denied having anything to do with it.

"I couldn't top that!" he told Welsh, laughing it off.

The NYPD was not taking chances. A second incarnation
of the old Pizza Squad was dispatched 24-7 to President Street
in the aftermath of the shooting. Plainclothesmen kept watch
on Joey's apartment on Fourteenth Street, jam-packed with foot
traffic, a bitch for surveillance. To keep Joey from causing any
more trouble on President Street, his parole officer reminded
him that it was a violation to associate with known criminals,
but Joey still snuck down to President Street for early-morning
visits. The cops slacked off after a while. They weren't too
worried if one hood popped off another.

Pal Joey

In the summer of 1971, Joe Colombo rolled out the red carpet for *The Godfather*. His men ensured that Staten Islanders wouldn't disturb the filming of the lavish wedding scene. A few blocks from President Street, the Gallo gang heckled the low-budget MGM production of *The Gang That Couldn't Shoot Straight*, inspired by columnist Jimmy Breslin's reporting of the Gallo-Profaci war, showcasing a group of ragtag gangsters, including a pet lion and Beppo the Dwarf.

"Smile pretty for the camera, motherfuckers!" yelled Mondo the Midget, heckling his counterpart Hervé Villechaize, a dwarf dubbed over to give him a tough Brooklyn accent.

Joey's fictionalized on-screen debut wasn't the honorable Michael Corleone, stepping up to the mantle of don to obey his family duty, or the psychotic killer Tommy Udo, stalking the night in search of kicks. It was a bumbling hood named Kid Sally Palumbo.

Right after the December 1971 release of *The Gang That Couldn't Shoot Straight*, Joey got a visit from former Pizza

Squad detective Eddy Lambert, who told Joey that he'd met Jerry Orbach, the guy who played Kid Sally. Bronx-born with great hair, Jerry played the type of characters that Joey usually went for, Mack the Knife in *The Threepenny Opera* and gambler Sky Masterson in the gangster musical *Guys and Dolls*, making it all the more difficult to accept Jerry's stint on the big screen as Kid Sally, a real jerk-off. A sit-down was scheduled for the Queen Restaurant, a Gallo hangout on Court Street.

"It appealed to me," Jerry told the *New York Post*, "because I wanted to find out how right or wrong I had portrayed the man. I found out that I had been very wrong, because in the story he had been a boob, a clown—and this was a very intelligent man."

"Hey, Punchy," said Joey, calling one of the boys over to the table. "You see the one over there? With the white? That's the guy that played me in the movie. You know what? We should have broke his legs. Just to teach him to be a better actor."

Joey asked Jerry's tall and voluptuous wife, Marta, if she preferred Camus or Sartre. Marta "almost fell into a plate of spaghetti," she told the press.

"I said I preferred Camus," Marta revealed to famed columnist Earl Wilson. "Joey said he thought Camus was suicidal and Joey liked survivors. I challenged him on Camus being suicidal. He referred to the auto accident in which Camus was killed and said that anybody who went in a car with somebody driving that fast was suicidal."

"Listen, Italian girl," said Joey. "Someday I'm going to come over and I'm going to eat your goddamn spaghetti. Will your actor be there? Will you be there, actor?"

"I realized I hadn't had spaghetti on Sunday since I lived

with my father and grandmother," Marta told the *Post*. "Joey was Neapolitan and I'm Sicilian, and even though the Neapolitans and Sicilians may hate each other, they understand each other."

"There's a corner of Italian background in me," Marta told *Time*, "that was ready to be activated. The first day I laid eyes on Joey, it was like being with my father. Joey sensed it, and my family sensed it. After that we were with him almost every day. And if we didn't see him, he'd call up and ask where the hell we were."

Joey forged a friendship with the Orbachs over late nights in their spacious Chelsea brownstone. Quoted by society columnist Charlotte Curtis in a feature for *Harper's Bazaar*, "The Last Delicious Days of Joey Gallo," Marta revealed how Joey opened up in her all-electric kitchen. "He'd sit around my kitchen with those sad, sad eyes. He wanted to talk about things—everything."

"You don't understand, Momma," said Joey. "I gotta get off."

Sitting in the Orbachs' kitchen, where restaurant-size pots and pans hung from the brick wall and the occasional Smithfield ham hung from the ceiling, Joey knew he needed to get his kicks, to plug into the thing that made life worth living. He'd run the gamut, from jazz impresario to hash-smoking beatnik to fiery revolutionary, but all he got was ten years in the can and a pack of hit men on him.

"Joey compressed time with us," said Jerry, "because he knew in the back of his head that he might not have much time, that he could go at any minute. Consequently, a minute spent talking to Joey was like an hour spent with someone else."

Joey told Jerry he didn't like it when Marta talked like a

man because then he'd have to treat her like a man. He didn't want to stop treating her like a woman.

"Joey was a terribly sexy person," Marta told *Time*, saying that Joey called her Momma, "or sometimes the Big Job." He once told her to shut up, but "in our family and our world," said Marta, "women are bright and they talk too, and he began to understand."

Getting hip to the ways of society, Joey hit the town with the Orbachs. His social debut was on a snowy night at actor Ben Gazzara's dinner party. Joey told former Copa girl Janice Rule how much the boys in the can enjoyed her flicks. Lounge singer and piano man Buddy Greco showed up in a pair of knickers.

"Jesus Christ," said Joey. "You've been singing for thirty-five years. What kind of an outfit is that?"

Greco invited Joey to his opening at the St. Regis.

Joey took his mother to Sardi's. He was ready to assume his place on the wall with the rest of the caricatures.

"Do you know anyone who steals dogs?" asked Marta.

"What kind of dog do you want?" asked Joey.

Joey called on Mrs. Peter Stone, the wife of the famous playwright, at her ritzy apartment. Somebody had kidnapped her dog. Joey pegged her as the victim of a dognapping ring. He sent the Greek to comb seedy Times Square to find the pooch. Mrs. Stone thanked Joey with comp tickets to her husband's new Broadway show, *Sugar*.

At the opening night of *Night Watch*, Joey watched actress Joan Hackett play a stuttering socialite whose husband was driving her insane so he could run off with her money. Joey sent her a big floral arrangement with an attached card—"Dear Joan, you're a good broad."

" 'Broad' is a word I would never accept from anybody but Joe," said Joan.

Joey phoned Joan's sunny Central Park West apartment to chat, interrupting her wine and omelet lunch with *New York Times* reporter Guy Flatley, who added Joey to his puff piece on Joan—"an ex-convict whose miraculous transformation from underworld figure to self-made super-philosopher has captured Joan's fancy."

"Everyone talked about it," said Mrs. Richard Clurman, socialite. "It was the thing to do. You'd go somewhere, and people would say, 'Have you met Joey Gallo?' and it was like Stravinsky and Yevtushenko. If you hadn't met him, you weren't in."

"Our relationship has been described as like Hemingway hanging out with bullfighters or Mailer hanging out with prizefighters," Marta told the *New York Post*, "but this is obscene because we weren't role playing. We hung out with Joey 'cause we thought he was such a great person."

On Sunday afternoons, the Orbachs hosted invitation-only brunches, wanting their closest friends to meet Joey. "When we entertain," Jerry told the *Post*, "we go for a loose, informal dinner and a poker game upstairs afterward." Marta set the tone in jeans and an old sweater. Instead of Jerry's famed egg, ham, and cheese bake, it was spaghetti, just how the guest of honor liked it. Everybody sat at the big table, sipped red wine, and picked at the green salad.

Joey sat at the poker table and eyeballed the playwright Neil Simon. He sat on the white brocade sofa and made outrageous statements in leisurely political debates. He dug President Nixon almost as much as LBJ, a tough guy who had a real set of balls.

"He was as bright and interesting as people said," remarked socialite D. D. Ryan. "He'd done a lot of thinking. It was nice to talk with someone who had the time to think."

Joey held court at the table in the back left corner of Elaine's on the Upper East Side and gave proprietress Elaine Kaufman "the eye-lock," she remembered. The spot for Manhattan's who's who, from filmmaker Woody Allen to Joey's new pals, Ben Gazzara and novelist Bruce Jay Friedman, Elaine's was the after-hours home for the literary elite, a place to rub elbows with Gay Talese, dapper author of the recent bestseller *Honor Thy Father*, his portrait of New York City's underworld as seen through the Bonanno Family, with mentions of the Gallo brothers.

After a few drinks, the warm glow and the book jackets by the bathroom made an aspiring writer like Joey feel that he'd already made it, that he deserved to be in the company of heavyweights like Norman Mailer, who had already inched in on Joey's creative turf.

In the late 1960s, Mailer and his two pals hung out in a Village dive, drinking and carousing while pretending to be gangsters.

"We go into bars and do fights or wild conversations and let whatever happens, happen," Mailer told vérité filmmaker D. A. Pennebaker. "You can see it's brutal, but when we get it right it's going someplace. We're the Gallo brothers now. We've been hiding out."

Mailer put the act on film, resulting in the underground arthouse romp *Wild 90*. "After a few moments, one begins to long for the Gallo brothers," said *New York Times* critic Renata Adler.

Joey needed to get in on the action. He mulled over that

prison black comedy he wanted to do. Shortly before Christmas, he said he had to get his head straight before getting down to work, but it wasn't easy to settle into a writing routine with Colombo's hit men after him. Joey figured he could make it happen with Marta's help.

At an Orbach brunch, Joey spilled his spaghetti on Viking publisher Thomas Guinzburg. Guinzburg gave him a book deal. Joey brought his bodyguards for the meet at Viking Press. "There's something suicidal about publishers," he told the Greek, "paying a lot of greens for the big nothing."

Some days Joey went to the Chelsea townhouse. Other days Marta arrived at his Union Square pad. Joey wanted the book to be a darkly comic work of fiction, based around a convict named Slick. Telling Marta about his own prison life, he said all of the stories about his recruiting a black gang in Auburn were "a myth," something to shake up the boys in Brooklyn. Joey pointed at the tall buildings outside his window, perfect position for a sniper.

"Hey, that's the Texas Book Depository," said Marta.

"Finally you know what it's like to try to stay alive," said Joey.

An MGM production exec reportedly came to Joey's apartment to discuss the script version of what had been tentatively titled "A-Block." "In A-Block," Joey pitched to A. H. Weiler, *New York Times* film critic, "the central character comes out on top in every situation and is actually *comfortable* in a prison environment. The film will be a spoof of authentic prison conditions, not an exposé—we've had enough of them."

"I'm very sentimental about my teeth," said Joey, "because they saved my life a few times."

He didn't use them much around Jeffie. She never cooked. His mother thought she was starving him. Umberto came up to Joey's apartment to stash boxes of food, bought whole-sale, dozens of steaks and pork chops, and eighteen bags of fruit.

"I can't, Pop," snapped Jeffie. "You don't understand. I can't take it anymore! I can't—he's going to drive me insane. I don't want it. Where am I going to put all this fucking food?"

Joey got in the habit of going up for dinner at Sina's pent-house, two floors above Joey. Sina worked on the main floor at the dentist's office. Joey had come in with bone damage. Sina had a nice spread, wall-to-wall carpeting, a brand-new bookcase, a new armoire. Joey reportedly tried to saw off an end of it so the TV would fit.

On Christmas Eve, Joey had a big tree brought up from the peddlers on the street. Carols played on the hi-fi as Joey decorated it with tinsel. He went two floors down to get out of a previous engagement. Jeffie opened her present, a zodiac charm with an inlaid diamond, indulging her interest in as-trology. It was the wrong sign. The doomed couple ended up screaming at each other.

"Fuck you," said Jeffie, "and fuck Christmas."

Joey took back his present and went upstairs. He took Sina and her daughter out for dinner with Umberto. They went to midnight Mass. Joey wanted to celebrate Christmas Eve that way forever.

Kid Blast didn't have any use for showbiz people or their ilk, but Joey's absences from President Street put him in the hot seat on sit-downs, giving him a chance to command his own carefully tailored brand of diplomacy, taken from the best of his brothers.

Larry always had a rep as a straight shooter, strictly business in a perfectly knotted black tie, a sensible guy you could deal with. Blast updated the look with a brown double-breasted blazer. He slicked back his long hair and trimmed his thick sideburns below the ears, courtesy of a barber he brought onto President Street. His nails were immaculate.

The wild blood streaking through Joey flowed through Blast, but no one knew for sure what wheeled behind his Elvis shades. Blast worked the unpredictability card to advantage in the Colombo peace negotiations, ongoing, like President Nixon's strategy to end the war in Vietnam—"the madman theory."

According to informants, while sitting in the back of Roy Roy's, a President Street social club, in November 1971, Blast laid it out for Gallo-turned-Colombo Nick Bianco. Peace had a price. One hundred and fifty thousand dollars, the share of greens that the Gallos had been cheated out of since Larry's death. Bianco said it was impossible. Blast said it was fine. The Gallos didn't want to make peace anyway.

The word was that Joey was making one or two hundred button men in the Gallo gang, including blacks and Puerto Ricans, which meant that the Colombos lived in fear of not knowing from which way they'd be killed. Bianco left President Street wondering just how crazy the Gallos were. Blast kept him on his toes, but insiders didn't expect the Colombos to break out the guns.

As one Gallo source leaked to the FBI, top guys in the Colombo family were happy to see Joe Colombo out of the picture, and "anyone thinking about moving against the Gallo crew at this time has to be made aware the Gallo faction will respond forcefully." All the Gallos wanted was to be left alone, free to control their strip of Brooklyn and run it for themselves with no hassles.

There was only obstacle, Junior Persico, the last legitimate force to deal with in the family. In the latest tangle, a Gallo shot Junior's bodyguard, Apples, in the gut. Apples had a load of liquor in him and wouldn't go down, hanging on until he got dumped in front of a Coney Island Hospital, where he lasted through to recovery.

Months later, on January 24, 1972, Apples was finally put down. Not by the Gallos, but Feds, who threw him in the big house in Atlanta for six years as a co-conspirator on the old Akers job, ending a decade of hung juries, delayed sentences, mistrials, and appeals in one of the longest-running cases in the history of the Eastern District of New York. Junior went with him.

This time, the slick lawyers fell through on Junior's appeal, rejected by the court on March 15, 1972, with the statement that the "defendant's attempt to demonstrate prosecutorial misconduct is frivolous and that a new trial need not be granted." For a truck full of cheap linen, Junior got fourteen years. The Gallos were home free.

—◁◁◁◁ᛘ▷▷▷▷—

On March 16, the Orbachs hosted Joey and Sina's wedding at their Chelsea townhouse. The ring was a four hundred dollar diamond job from Cartier. The wedding cake had an enormous front piece of the bride and groom. Columnist Earl Wilson sent one of his guys down from the *Post* to cover the event.

Rev. William Glenesk of the Village Presbyterian Church performed the ceremony. Young and handsome, with black, short-cropped hair, his notable gigs included the sublime eulogy of Lenny Bruce—"He was a man, uptight against an artificial world, who shattered its faces and its hypocrisy"—and the absurd marriage ceremony of Village folkie Tiny Tim and "Miss Vicki," performed in front of a live television audience on *The Johnny Carson Show*.

At the last minute, Joey decided he didn't want his driver, Cousin Tony, to be the best man. He wanted David Steinberg, the famous comedian. Cousin Tony didn't bother sticking around.

Allan Jones, a tenor who played the straight man in two Marx Brothers films, sang a rendition of the Lord's Prayer. Sina wore a simple white dress. Joey wore a double-breasted gray suit with a polka dot tie.

"Do you, Nina, take this man . . ."

"No, no, not Nina! Sina! Sina!"

"Let's do it again."

"Are we married yet?"

"No, not yet!"

"God is a tough customer!" cracked Joey. He had tears in his eyes after the service.

"You made a Christian out of me," he told Allan Jones. "I got religious, hearing you sing that."

The following evening, Joey looked onto the Hudson River

from the window of Allan's apartment on the West Side. He talked about all the years he lost staring across a prison yard.

On Saturday night, Joey took Sina and his mother out to the San Susan nightclub in Mineola, Long Island. Joey wanted to hear Jimmy Roselli, old-school Hoboken crooner. Fans called him Mozart to Sinatra's Salieri. Roselli sold records from the back of his car on Mulberry Street, unwilling to bow down to the mob to get famous. Joey heckled Roselli through-out the act. He got sloppy drunk and gave big wet kisses. Sit-ting at the other end of the bar were a few of the guys from President Street. Nobody in the gang congratulated him on his wedding. None of the Gallos had much of anything to say to Joey that night. It was daylight by the time Joey let the Greek chauffeur him home to Union Square. Roselli at the San Susan had been enough to give him a big hangover. He stared at the morning headline under *The Godfather* ad in the *New York Times*:

THE ORBACHS' PAL JOEY

Two weeks later, on Monday, April 3, *Voices* opened its Broadway previews at the Ethel Barrymore Theatre. The play starred Joey's stepdaughter, Lisa, making big headway as a child actor. The Orbachs booked a table at Sardi's to celebrate the opening. Joey didn't feel like going.

Outside the Ethel Barrymore under the lights of Broad-way, Joey smoked with his back to the wall and waited for his driver to pick him up and take him home. Two days later, the doorman buzzed Sina's penthouse. Delivery in the lobby. Sina said to send him up. Joey flipped out. He posted Pete the

Greek outside the elevator. The doors slid open. The Greek pulled a gun and choked the deliveryman. He handed over the package. It was a Tiffany ice bucket from Bruce J. Friedman, whose sons had played pool with Joey at the Orbachs' brunch.

Joey screamed at Sina for being so stupid. He threw her in a chair.

Sina didn't intend to take the shit Jeffie had put up with. "If this is what my life with you is going to be," she said, "you have to leave."

Joey couldn't move back downstairs. It was a wreck. Joey had torn up the wall-to-wall carpet with his bare hands to send back to Jeffie, along with all of the furniture.

Whacked

Opening night at the Copa and he knocked 'em dead on his first set, like Martin and Lewis in the old days. The greats. They didn't make guys like that anymore, but Don Rickles was no slouch. They called him the Merchant of Venom. Mr. Warmth. He got ready for the second act when a couple of tough guys approached him backstage with a message. The boss was in the audience tonight. The boss had a sensitive nature. Rickles had a rep for being insensitive. Fine with the boss, so long as Rickles didn't fling any of that funny stuff in his direction.

Any seasoned performer at the Copa knew the stakes on underworld characters. Those who didn't could look to that time when Jerry Lewis was working the bar crowd in between shows. A big guy with a bull chest, who didn't think Jerry was all that funny, growled, "Why don't you knock off that shit and shut the fuck up?" Jerry cracked a zinger comeback, "That's what happens when cousins get married." The big guy told Jerry he'd knock out his teeth.

Dean Martin promptly apologized for his partner Jerry,

who was a little green to the rule: *Never* joke with boys from the Syndicate. Especially when that guy was the hated and feared Albert Anastasia, the Butcher of Brooklyn.

Only Rickles had an irreverent streak. He thought about what the tough guys had told him and figured, "That's like painting a bull's-eye on yourself. A guy sits in the front row smoking a big cigar and surrounded by five bodyguards and I'm supposed to *ignore* him?"

Fuck 'em. He was the Mad Emperor of Comedy. A bullet-headed matador. He stepped into the ring and took his applause. The joint was packed with who's whos. Nightlife maven Earl Wilson. Actor Jerry Orbach. Comedian David Steinberg. Rickles worked over the room. First the Jews. Then the blacks. He scanned ringside for big cigars. Out there with some showbiz types was flat-topped Punchy. At another table was Russ Bufalino, boss of Erie, Pennsylvania. Rickles looked up to the long table on the top terrace and grinned. As Pete the Greek remembered, "I was told to be *very* careful what I said," cracked Rickles. "Particularly to those people on the upper balcony."

Everybody looked up. There was Crazy Joe Gallo in a blue pinstriped suit, flanked by bodyguards, and his wife and sister. Joey hadn't been to the Copa in ten years, since his shotgun-wedding road trip kickoff party, but they still treated him like a king. The maître d' gave him the best table. Busboys cleared the chicken chow mein. The manager sent over champagne, which was polished off quick. Joey grabbed the empty bottle from the ice bucket and stood up like he was going to hurl it on stage. Rickles covered his balding head with his arms and cowered. "Ma! Ma!"

The crowd roared. Christ, he was good. Joey couldn't

stop laughing the whole set. Rickles brought down the house. Joey's stepdaughter Lisa worked the floor. She'd been announced as one of the in-house celebrities tonight, fresh off her smash debut on Broadway in *Voices*. She thanked Earl Wilson for mentioning her in his *New York Post* column on her stepfather.

"Oh! Is Joey Gallo here?" asked Midnight Earl's wife. It was two in the morning and getting late, but she always wanted to meet a real gangster. Lisa took them up to the balcony to join the table, celebrating with cake and more champagne.

"I know all about you." said Joey. "You're the BW."

That was Earl's term for the Beautiful Wife. The BW noticed the big mole on his left cheek.

"Why, you're a diplomat!" she said.

Joey had learned about the BW when he went to Earl's office weeks before to talk about his future as a writer. He told Earl that his old life on President Street was over—"I'll never go back there. I think there's nothing out there for me but death."

Tonight, Joey told Wilson he'd be willing to spill the beans on the present Mob scene, which would be a scorcher given *The Godfather* hype.

"Tell your secretary to call me and we'll make an appointment. I don't like to talk on the phone."

A bottle got sent from a showbiz table. The cork popped. Joey drank up. Bubbles fizzled up the flute. The party moved to the round bar at the lounge. More champagne was sent over by the Irishman, six-four and balding. He was a dangerous guy, the muscle on Erie boss Bufalino, who came over to say hi to Joey. A diamond-inlaid Numero Uno button twinkled on his lapel.

"What're you doing with that?" cracked Joey. "You really believe in that bullshit league?"

Bufalino didn't think Joey was very funny. He walked away. The Irishman took Joey's arm.

"Joey, that's nothing to talk about here. Let's have a few drinks."

"Yeah, we'll have a few drinks."

"Joey, he's a *boss*."

"So he's a boss. So am I a boss. That make him any better than me? We're all equal. We're all supposed to be *brothers*."

The Greek stopped him before it got worse. "Joey, let's go to the table. Let's not have a beef."

Joey followed the Greek to the table with the girls. Edie, the Greek's girl, asked what was wrong.

"Nothing. We're all having a good time."

Don Rickles came over with his mother. One time at the Copa, his mother told Joey, "The only way you can talk to my Don is if you put the guns on the table." Five irons dropped on the table.

They talked for almost an hour tonight. They talked about Larry. Joey asked if Rickles remembered what had happened at the old Elegante.

It was getting late, about four in the morning. Busboys stacked up chairs. The place was clearing out. Joey told his other bodyguard, Bobby D, to take off and lay the broad he'd been angling. Jerry Orbach told David Steinberg he should come to the after-party, but Joey's best man had a noon appointment to play basketball at the YMCA. He cut out early. Maybe Jerry did too. Things were getting a little fuzzy with all the champagne sent over. Joey invited Rickles, but Rickles said good night. He was a little nervous at the prospect of an early morning with Joey, given what happened at the old Elegante.

—◦◦◦◦◦—

Joey's entourage piled from the Copa into the Greek's black Cadillac, the windows pasted with black and orange stickers from the Americans of Italian Descent, a rival organization to Colombo's League. Joey had met its head, Congressman Santangelo, the week before to offer services to the Italian people. They swapped watches as a good-faith token.

Around four thirty, the Greek cruised down the FDR along the East River. Light rain wiped off the windshield. The Greek hoped Joey would change his mind, but Joey made him turn off downtown. He had his mind set on Su Ling's.

"We just ate Chinese food," said the Greek.

Wise guys had been hitting the spots for chow mein and Scotch, but Joey insisted the Greek make the slow ride through Chinatown. Sanitation trucks cleared exotic garbage off the narrow streets. Yellow signs lit up Chinese characters at a few dive noodle houses. Su Ling's was closed. Joey told the Greek to hit Mulberry Street.

"*Luna's* you want to go and eat at?"

"Luna's, Greek."

The crescent moon over the Luna was off, but Joey was hungry, leaving the Greek to figure out someplace else. He headed a few blocks north on Mulberry Street, quiet and dark save a blue-and-white sign lighting up the corner of Hester:

Umberto's
Clam House

It looked a little like Luigi's Seafood and Cocktails in *Kiss of Death*, where psycho killer Tommy Udo, in his black suit, black shirt, and white tie, enjoyed a last meal before he stepped out under the lighted sign and got gunned down on the sidewalk.

Umberto's was brand-new, with big arched windows and a fresh whitewash. Joey's sister Carmella said it looked nice.

"Ask if the broiled shrimps and scungilli are worth eating in this dump," said Joey.

The Greek stopped the Caddy and rolled down the window. He nodded to Matty the Horse, standing in the drizzle. Next to the Horse was a thick guy with a fat neck. The Greek asked about the scungilli. The Horse saw Joey and the girls in the backseat.

"Everything's good," said the Horse.

"Pull around the corner," said Joey. "Find a place to park."

The Greek went around the block. A space opened up right in front on Hester Street.

Umberto's gleamed with white tiles, brightly lit. Fishing nets and lifesavers hung on the wall. Crowded given the hour, five in the morning. A collection of late-nighters sat at the square butcher-block tables. Four men in work clothes. An Asian couple. Two college girls on spring break staying with family. A few night crawlers sitting at tables and the wooden bar stools at the clam bar.

Joey walked the length of the restaurant to a table at the right rear so he could face the back door leading onto Mulberry. The Greek sat beside him, putting some flesh on his left. Sina sat directly across the table, her daughter to her right, close by the coat stand. Edie sat across from Carmella. They wore elegant, ankle-length jersey dresses. The college girl sitting behind them thought Sina was pretty. The waiter put down the bread and menus, then came back to take their orders. Joey turned around in the wooden captain's chair and jerked his thumb at the Horse, sitting at the swivel barstool. At his side was a big guy with bad skin.

"Let him order for us," said Joey. "He'll know what's good. Right, Matty? You tell them what to bring."

The Horse didn't pay much notice. He ordered them boiled shrimp and scungilli salad. Double orders.

Sal, the cook, was pissed. A half hour until closing time, he was getting ready to pack up the clams and clean the fryer. Now he had to boil water, chop the parsley for the salad, squeeze on the lemon, and pour the oil. Plenty of garlic on the scungilli.

The table polished it off in a minute. Everybody was happy to be together after a great night out. The girls talked about how good the show was at the Copa. Joey said Rickles had come a long way. From a nobody at the Elegante to the head-liner at the Copa.

Joey wasn't a kid anymore, but ten years in the joint had left him a lot of living still to do. He could write that book. The one he wanted. He'd take the book deal and run. He didn't have a thing to lose doing it his way. No ghostwriter. He read more than any Ivy League jockey. He had crazy ideas.

His sister adored him. He had a gorgeous wife. His step-daughter loved him like a father. She liked wearing his peaked cap around the apartment. The boys on President Street? Didn't need 'em. Copa ringside? Sour. They didn't even have the Copa girls anymore. He didn't need the brunches, the columns in the papers. He had everything he needed.

He had a lot to live for.

Joey ordered up a second helping for everyone and left

to go take a leak. He made his way past the clam bar, down the black and white painted stairwell to a dark, cavernous cellar. Walking along the long corridor, he made his way to the men's room at the end. There were all kinds of doors that he couldn't figure out. He heard noises. Rustling sounds. Whispering. It didn't make any sense. Right in front of him was a huge metal door leading to a walk-in freezer. A guy could hide a lot of bodies in there. The place was like a tomb.

Back upstairs waiting for the food, Carmella leaned into the Greek—"I wonder what happened to him." Joey had been down in the john for five minutes already.

"What do you suppose he's doing down there?" asked Sina.

"Pete, why don't you take a look? See if he's okay."

"Ah come on, leave him alone. Can't a guy even go to the men's room now, for Chrissake?"

"But why would he take so long? I don't like it, Pete. I think you ought to go down there."

"Listen, Cam, I'm telling you—leave him alone. I know what I'm doing."

Joey finally emerged from the stairwell. He looked pale. He wasn't smiling when he sat down.

"Jesus," said Joey. "It's spooky down there."

Carmella gave him a kiss on the cheek.

"Well, happy birthday, brother."

He was forty-three.

The Horse got up from his stool and headed for the kitchen. The guy with the pimples didn't move from the counter. The glass backdoor opened and a man came in off Mulberry Street. It was 5:23AM. The college girl thought the man was handsome. Distinctive. Really tall. She looked down at her plate of seafood and heard a gunshot. Everybody in the place was ducking. The Greek too. Joey jumped up and knocked his sister down to the floor, then flung the butcher-block table on top of his wife and kid.

Glasses and plates, bottles of ketchup and Umberto's hot sauce crashed on top of them, all huddled under the thick wooden shield. Lisa screamed. Sina kept her coat over Lisa's head and told her to act dead and not look up no matter what happened. Joey drew fire away from the table by sprinting the length of the restaurant toward the front door. His left elbow shattered and the bullet dropped in the lining of his pinstripes. Still running. Bullets whizzed, chipping white cement off the walls. Two shots went through his coattails as he passed the jukebox. Another got him in the lower spine. He opened the glass door. Almost free. Then he got it in the back.

Joey leaned against the black Cadillac, pushed himself off, and staggered out into the middle of the intersection of Hester and Mulberry. He dropped on his back. Carmella ran out to hold her brother's head in her lap. There was no sign of blood. Joey's eyes were wandering, but he breathed in gasps. Three quarts of blood began filling up his chest. Bleeding on the inside.

This was it. The big finale.

Carmella's screams caught the attention of a radio car that happened to be cruising down Hester Street. The prowler pulled up as the Greek tossed away his .25 caliber Titan automatic. He might as well not have had it. The hit man slipped off in a getaway car. The cop ran to the intersection and looked down at the mole on the left side of the victim's face. The guy looked a lot like Richard Widmark. Or maybe the

Riddler on *Batman*. Maybe even a little like George Raft or Jimmy Cagney.

"Who is he?" asked the cop. "He looks familiar."

"It's my brother," cried Carmella. "Joey Gallo. Joe Gallo."

Joey's bright blue eyes glazed past his sister's tears toward the lighted sign of Umberto's.

The Godfather

Chief of Detectives Albert Seedman received the news in an early-morning call from his second-floor office at 240 Centre Street. Joe Gallo just "bought his" at Umberto's Clam House.

"Any suspects?"

"No, Chief."

"Tell the detectives down there not to talk to the press. I'll make a statement when I get there."

Chief Seedman put on his Fifth-Avenue-tailored button-down with the red cursive "Al" monogrammed on the cuff. The dark suit cut a block over his square shoulders, hiding the pearl-handled revolver. The onyx ring slid onto his right pinky. On his left ring finger, the diamond.

Driving out of his ranch house in Nassau County, the Chief lit his cigar and hit the Long Island Expressway toward Manhattan.

The dirty city was going to pot, up to its eyeballs in urban guerrillas throwing Molotov cocktails, Weathermen, and soldiers from the Black Liberation Army, who had taken credit for the killing of two cops outside an East Village luncheonette in

January. Given the glut of nutcase radicals, it made sense that a faction of his detectives was convinced that black revolutionaries offed Joe Colombo. They hadn't been around for the days of Murder, Inc., when tough guys like Anastasia perfected the art of gangland killing.

It was seven in the morning, but a big crowd had already gathered in the cold behind the crime-scene tape stretched across the intersection. One man dragged his sons out of bed and brought them over on the subway to view the morbid spectacle. This was history, he figured, something they could tell their sons about.

The networks rolled film as anchormen told a grisly tale of the mean streets. A few silk-tied armchair mobsters offered commentary on the sidelines.

"It's just like *The Godfather*. They filmed it down the block, you know. Yeah, Corleone got hit right over there. You seen *The Godfather*? Oh, you should. It's really good. And *The Gang That Couldn't Shoot Straight*? That was about Joey Gallo."

"If you ask me," said his pal, "a bodyguard is there to shoot. Not to get shot."

"I don't know why he even went there. It's just opened. You want decent food, you go to Vinnie's down the block."

Chief Seedman made his way under the tape into the sea of green-and-white Plymouth Furys outfitted with sirens. He stood next to Deputy Police Commissioner Robert Daley in the icy drizzle.

"He made a mistake, Crazy Joe did," said Daley. "He should have gone to bed last night."

Detectives jotted down the facts in notebooks. Yellow measuring tape stretched between overturned tables. The photo unit snapped the camera-ready bloodbath. The white tile floor was a mess of red chunks mixed with plate and glass shards. A guy who had a stake in the place was ready to clean up for lunch.

"How soon do you think I can reopen?"

"Why don't you shut up?" snapped the Chief. "If we get any trouble from you, we'll stay here a week."

Forensics checked the gore. It was ketchup and hot sauce.

The Latent Print Unit dusted white mineral powder on the glass of the side door onto Mulberry Street and rushed the stack of Polaroids to a guarded loft at 400 Broome Street, near headquarters. Detective Scalice flipped through to see which prints looked promising.

The Feds used newfangled computers, but Scalice preferred a magnifying glass and bloodshot eyes. "A machine can't make the identifications we make," said Scalice. He pulled the thick stack of mob prints from the special files of worn metal cabinet, laid out on 8 × 10-inch cards.

Chief Seedman got the Police Engineering Unit on the big board. They neatly drew a ruled Umberto's diagram, marking bullets by the large square indicating the kitchen area, the straight line showing the location of the clam bar and the round circles indicating table locations.

"A flip chart with neat clear diagrams is a modern management technique to make it look like you know what you're doing," said the Chief. "That's very important when you don't have a damn thing to go on."

—◁▥▥ʃ∿▥▥▷—

Allie Boy Persico stepped out into the crisp spring air of Blue Mountain Manor, his brother's horse farm in Saugerties, in upstate New York, eager to live the life of a country gentleman. The morning light mixing with the smell of manure was enough to make him want to kick back with a cold one, maybe go fishing. He had a lot of living to catch up on after a lifetime behind bars in the New York State penal system.

Thirty years before, at six in the morning, the cops got a call that "they got him." They were directed to a twenty-six-year-old dock sweeper, fresh out of five years in Sing Sing on robbery and assault, shot four times in the back and neck and left face down in the Carroll Street gutter where he belonged. Junior was picked up on the homicide. An eight-state alarm went out for Allie Boy. For two weeks Allie Boy went on the lam, but as the eldest of the notorious Persico brothers, he had a duty to his little brother.

Allie Boy hired an attorney to arrange his surrender and on March 16, 1951 turned himself in to Captain Terranova of the Seventeenth Detective Division. He pled guilty to second-degree murder. Allie Boy got twenty to life. He took his time like a man while Junior worked his way up the ranks of the Profaci Family.

Now Junior was in jail, and while Allie Boy was ready to strap on the Lugers and carry the mantle for the Persico brothers, he didn't want to start blasting Gallos and jeopardize Junior's appeal with a lot of bad press. When the court rejected the appeal, Allie Boy loaded up. He had plenty of time to fish later. Now came the hunt.

One by one, Persico soldiers slinked upstate to the Snake's farm, deep in the hills of Ulster County. Like Johnny Bath Beach said, laying low in Miami Beach until the heat blew over, "a lot of funny things are happening with the Gallos, and something is going to have to be done with these people."

There would be no hit parade on this one, the usual list of targets in order of importance.

All Gallos were to be exterminated. No reprieves would be granted. No permission or clearance was needed for the hits.

This was a Colombo problem, and if members of another family involved themselves, Allie Boy had prior permission to kill them. He told the Persico crew not to go home at night and to stay in groups of three and four. No private jobs, no robberies, no hijackings until all Gallos were dead. No one would go hungry. The Persicos stashed up enough money to support a long war, and when the Gallos were dead in their graves, selected kids who participated in hits would be eligible for membership in the Brugad. The Borgata. The Family. Persicos needed to do the biggest part of the work so when the Colombo Family reorganized, Persicos would emerge as the dominant crew and take the biggest share of rewards.

Times had changed in the thirty years he'd been behind bars, but Allie Boy hadn't. He was taking the Colombos back to the old days, back when the ranks were free of the undesirables who had infested President Street. He'd blast the hippies, blacks, Puerto Ricans, and Gallos out of Red Hook. A dozen rifles. Two shotguns. Hundreds of rounds of ammo. Forty firework-bombs that looked and sounded just like hand grenades, good to smoke Gallos out of President Street. The rifles were well calibrated on the farm, tested in rounds of target practice.

Allie Boy got in the passenger seat of the main car. Charlie the Moose stepped in the crash car with the guns. If any Gallos pulled a roadside ambush, the Moose would plow right into them and start blasting. Gerry Lang got in the driver's seat next to Allie Boy and turned on the ignition.

GANG WAR COULD BE A ROUGH ONE

New York Times
APRIL 12, 1972

The odds favored the Colombos in terms of sheer man-power, a hundred and eighteen committed members, reported NYPD Intelligence, but with the boss still in a coma in his split-level home on Eighty-fifth Street, the team lacked the proper leadership. Neither of the acting bosses, Joe Yack and Vincent Aloi, had "the experience or the temperament to be a wartime leader," said the *New York Times*. Junior was a groomed warlord, but he had been sidelined in the Atlanta pen, forcing him to give orders through Allie Boy, who visited on a regular basis. If Allie Boy didn't step up to the plate, some of the old Profaci captains might have to come out of retirement. Harry Fontana. Johnny Bath Beach. Sally the Sheik. Bad guys. Heavy hitters.

"On the other side, the Gallo group is missing two of the three Gallo brothers," continued the *Times*, "but is still strong enough to cause a lot of damage."

Kid Blast was the wild card. His only action had been from the sidelines, a decade before. He wasn't a negotiator like Larry. He wasn't as aggressive as Joey. Then again, the papers said, he was smarter than both. He had spent a lot of time behind the chessboard, training to master the ancient game of combat.

"Both sides have the men and the guns to make it the bloodiest internal Mafia conflict in many years," concluded the *Times*.

Straphangers shoved their way onto the subway, checking the score in the tabloids.

5TH GANG SLAYING

New York Post
APRIL 11, 1972

Even tough guys watched their mouth around thick Gennaro Ciprio. As one Federal agent described him, he was "a dangerous man who could have done a lot of damage in any war unless he was hit first." After Boss Colombo got shot at the Unity Day Rally, hot-blooded Ciprio went berserk, swinging at black men in a rampage. A better cook than a bodyguard, he didn't stop the bullet that felled his boss, but fixed a mean red sauce in stints as the top chef at his restaurant, Gennaro's Feast Specialties. At two forty-five in the morning, sixty-nine hours after Crazy Joe was whacked, Ciprio stepped from the Feast to move his rental car. Across Eighty-sixth Street, a sniper picked him off from the rooftop of Valo Frocks dress shop.

6 BODIES IN 12 DAYS

Daily News
APRIL 12, 1972

Coming in at 5 feet 9 inches, three hundred pounds, was a small-time loan shark, Frank Ferriano, who was found behind a shanty in a parking lot by the Holland Tunnel with a bashed-in head and a slug in his shoulder. On him was a hundred bucks, a wristwatch, a bus driver's license, and work papers for his janitor job in the Elizabeth, New Jersey, school system.

7TH MOB SLAYING

New York Post
APRIL 12, 1972

Hours after they buried Crazy Joe, jewel thief and Colombo wannabe Richard Grossman was unwrapped from black plastic and removed from the trunk of a 1961 Dodge Dart. The cops found him thanks to an anonymous tipster, calling in to say, "This one is for Joey Gallo."

"We cannot permit the streets of this city to become a battleground for gang warfare," Police Commissioner Patrick Murphy said at a press conference. Chief Inspector Michael Codd added if the war didn't stop, "innocent persons could be killed by a stray bullet."

GANGLAND FIGURE FOUND SLAIN; CITY'S GANG-STYLE MURDERS RISE TO 8

New York Times
APRIL 20, 1972

Clad in a brown leather jacket, bookie David Wolosky was found sprawled in front of Beth Israel Hospital on First Avenue, DOA, with gunshot wounds to the chest and lung. The tip of his right pinky was missing. Perhaps a Sicilian message, an underworld code from *The Godfather*, but NYPD Detective Foresta said, "The little finger? That's nothing. Maybe it got shot off, or maybe it got caught in the door."

Bodies dropped like flies. The Mets lost three in a row to

the Astros in a brutal summer at Shea. The Yankees slumped in the worst losing streak of the season, while hits racked up across the city, from William Della Russo, shot three times in front of the crowded Georgy Girl bar on New Utrecht Avenue in Brooklyn, to Rosario Stabile, a truck dispatcher found dead in a car near Prospect Park.

Tabloids hung the bodies on Gallos and Colombos, but behind the hype, the score was still 1–1 in the Gallo-Colombo war. The Ciprio hit turned out to be an inside job. Colombos popped him off for being a Gallo double agent. Grossman was a wash, not "for Joey Gallo," like the tipster said. The body was in the trunk before Joey even got killed. Gang war was a good chance to trim the fat on old beef, opening the door for families to get some hits out of the way.

In his first major news profile, the *New York Times* credited Kid Blast with patience in the four months since his brother was gunned down, claiming that Red Hook saw it as "not cowardice but merely prudence" that Blast sat it out on President Street. "The food is rich and good at this headquarters, Brooklyn detectives say, but Gallo still manages to stay trim—and to find time for female companionship." He was portrayed in a teen-idol picture to complement the puff piece, offering a nice side angle of his chops, just the right size to cut out and paste on a trading card.

<hr />

The Neapolitan Noodle was good for a meet, a nice Italian restaurant tucked away on Manhattan's Upper East Side. A new place, only two weeks old, it was off the radar from the usual Colombo hangouts, which were completely staked out. The street wasn't heavily trafficked, and if by chance a cop walked by, it would be too hard to make identifications. The place was basement level and didn't have good visibility through the front windows.

Allie Boy had checked it out well in advance, taking no chances with the heat all over him. He couldn't piss without getting a federal indictment, like the one he was slapped with for making false statements on a government-insured loan, delivered to the farm by eight carloads of FBI men and New York state troopers, just as he was rolling out to give a hurting on the Gallos. They seized the stash in the barn and added "receiving firearms in interstate commerce" to his federal shit list. His lieutenant Gerry Lang got busted on fireworks possession for the grenades.

In the four months since the raid, Allie Boy hadn't even gotten a good shot at any of the Gallos. The Pizza Squad was back on President Street, offering the best security force a taxpayer could buy. Colombos hadn't been able to replenish the war coffers with the Feds knocking out their gambling rings, leaving Allie Boy hungry. He sat with Gerry and had a few drinks at the end of the kidney-shaped bar while they waited for their table. Joining them was Junior's pride and joy, Little Allie Boy.

By nine o'clock, the small bar area was packed with a Friday night crowd, including Charlie the Moose and two of Frank Fusco's boys, coming in separately over ten-minute intervals, just to be safe. They all stood at the bar until the table was ready. Allie Boy and Gerry got up from the bar stools, which were quickly taken by two kosher meat wholesalers, glad to take a load off after the long week.

The host took the Colombos to their big table in back. The waiter offered them the wine list, with plenty of good bottles from the big rack dividing the dining area and the bar.

First the wine, then food, then business. There was a lot to bring to the table.

Directly uptown on Pleasant Avenue, the Lucchese Family was making a fortune on wholesale heroin. They operated the whole enterprise like clockwork. Poppy brokers in Asia. Processing plants in Europe. Smuggling routes to bring the white powder into the city. Cutting rooms in the tenements to whack it up. Blacks to deal in Harlem. Political connections to keep the heat off their back. If the supply ran out, they counted on detectives from the Special Investigations Unit who were stealing dope seized from the French Connection and selling it back to the dealers wholesale.

The Colombo Family needed to start thinking about the future. Little Allie Boy's generation was tired of not getting in on the action. They grew up on the Stones and street fighting. They weren't afraid of junk and weren't going to let anyone stand in their way. Don Corleone was shot for the same reason. The kids had their heads all full of that *Godfather* shit.

Frank Fusco's boys didn't agree. Colombos needed to stick with gambling, an honorable vice, but the drug business would destroy the family. Maybe not now, but in the years to come. Whatever heat Colombos felt now would be tenfold on that white powder. The Gallo matter would pass. Nobody gave a damn about the Gallos. The city was better off without them. Once they were dead in the grave, things would cool. Business would come back to normal.

Back at the bar, the meat wholesalers talked shop. Sheldon Epstein managed Empire Veal and Lamb in the Bronx. Max Tekelch and Leon Schneider were with Flushing Meats in Brooklyn. Jack Forem owned the Famous Meat Market in Coney Island. One of their daughters was engaged to a guy who worked at the Noodle. It seemed like a great place to take the wives, gathered at the other end, right by the loner who had just walked in.

The loner was short and stocky, middle-aged, with thick black hair down to his shoulders. It looked like a wig. He was new in town, just in for a short stint from Vegas. He plunked down a ten-dollar bill for a Scotch and water. He sipped it slow and listened in on the conversation by the wine rack. They sounded like a couple of Brooklyn guys. They all got up from the bar. Their table was ready, reserved for nine thirty.

Outside on Seventy-ninth Street, a Colombo capo was late for the meet. He had a taste for black leather trench coats. According to the *New York Post*, he made his way under the green-and-white awning of the Noodle and walked down the steps from the sidewalk. Opening the door, he saw a long-haired freak pull two long-barreled .38s on a group of guys heading for their table.

Everybody was screaming. A guy grabbed his wife and pulled her down behind the table. The hit man stood there firing, nine shots, slow and calculated.

The capo turned around and ran, knowing he might not be so lucky the next time around.

MOB WAR NOW PERILS PUBLIC

Daily News
AUGUST 15, 1972

"Max Telech's widow would be sickened at *The Godfather* and consider Mario Puzo a writer of hard-core pornography.

She would be correct. Just as correct as she would be in saying Jimmy Breslin's *The Gang That Shouldn't Shoot Straight* was the product of demented thinking," wrote Jimmy Breslin in his *Newsday* column. "*The Gang That Couldn't Shoot Straight* shoots your husband in the back in a restaurant."

Gangster chic was dead.

At his morning press conference at City Hall, Mayor Lindsay, reeling from his ill-fated bid for the Democratic nomination for president, answered for the actions of his former appointees, saying, "The recent murder of innocent citizens by gangland executioners is an outrage which demands that the romanticization of the mob must be stopped and the gangsters run out of town."

The Mayor passed the buck to Police Commissioner Patrick Murphy, charging him to do everything within his power to "see to it that this city is no place for mobsters to do business."

The FBI gave him a hand. Murphy needed all the help he could get after the recent revelations of the Knapp Commission, which detailed the unsavory activities of his Sixth Narcotics Force in East Harlem, who had been trading heroin and cocaine to junkie informants in exchange for power tools and a minibike. One of the detectives handed over a wish list: two bottles each of Smirnoff, Harvey Bristol Cream, and Jack Daniel's, all for his daughter's bridal shower. Another told his addict he wanted smokes.

"I don't want Pall Mall, either. Parliament, you know."

"What about Winston?"

"No, I don't know anybody that smokes Winston."

Heading over to President Street, an FBI agent finally made good on Crazy Joe's old request to get him some

Colombo mug shots. One of Junior's detective cousins had been able to get the Persicos all the Gallo mug shots for easy reference, stashed away in a family bible. "They know what *we* look like," complained Joey, "but we don't know what *they* look like."

Gathering the gang together, the agent showed a pile of Colombos. "These are the guys you're after," he said, then compared the stack of mug shots to photos of the Noodle victims. "These are pictures of businessmen. You don't shoot them."

<hr />

The opening scene with the big wedding just blew him away, all that music, honor, and dancing. "So on the money," said Sammy the Bull, "it was crazy." Even the mob stuff. The part about going to the mattresses took him back to the old days of the Profaci war, to when he and Tommy Snake and Lenny the Mole got in a barroom shootout with some Gallos over on New Utrecht Avenue. "It was like a cowboy movie," remembered the Bull. "Totally unbelievable."

And what that Turk pulled, the kidnapping and the drugs and the hit on Old Man Corleone? "Completely ruthless," said Joey the Hit Man, showing up on the *David Susskind Show* with a voice modulator and black ski mask. "He doesn't give a fuck."

The Bull could give a lesser fuck about the fedoras sold at the souvenir shops, or *The Godfather* board game or *The Godfather* spaghetti hawked by the Paramount merchandising staff, or even the proposed *Godfather Pizza* franchises, hero shops, bakeries, and lemon ice stands. Leave that for the tourists. On-screen in five separate theaters across mid-Manhattan, this was it. Lines wrapped around the block.

"I left that movie stunned," admitted the Bull. "I mean, I floated out of the theater. Maybe it was fiction, but for me, then, that was our life. It was incredible. I remember talking to a multitude of guys, made guys, everybody, who felt exactly the same way."

⚊⚊⚊⚊

"That lens? Does it make me look like John Derek?"

"No," said *New York Post* photographer Frank Leonardo, setting up the shot. "No way. Are you Sicilian?"

"Neapolitan," said Coppola. "There *are* Neapolitan gangsters. Al Capone. Vito Genovese. Luciano."

Thick, with a full beard and wild black hair, thirty-three-year-old Francis Ford Coppola looked the part of the young genius in his orange racing scarf, unkempt brown corduroy suit, and loose socks. He sat in the lobby of the St. Regis Hotel, where three weeks before, in the midst of a blizzard, the orchestra played Nino Rota's waltz at *The Godfather* opening-night party. Eighteen bouncers in double-breasted pinstripe suits kept anything funny from happening. Sitting in the invitation-only crowd was Sidney Korshak, Chicago's man in Hollywood, having taken Don Corleone's advice that "a lawyer with his briefcase can steal more than a hundred men with guns."

In the weeks since, his film bringing in a million a day at the box office, Coppola dismissed any intention of glamorizing the mob, stating that Puzo's story was pure fiction.

"I don't think those people were or are like that—romantic figures. I think they're *awful* people. I don't think there's a quarter of an ounce of loyalty among them. I hated the guys I was reading about, I really did. It just struck me that this sense of honor, taking care of your own, is what this country doesn't have. What if the United States of America took care of its people the way Don Corleone took care of his own? So to me, *The Godfather* is total fiction and metaphor. I never took it all that seriously in the first place."

THERE IS NO GODFATHER

New York Post
APRIL 6, 1972

Massapequa kids liked to throw the ball and skate around the circle in front of Mr. Gambino's modest yellow-brick home on Club Drive, a horseshoe strip of ranch houses with an ocean view. Preferring treats to tricks, the old man doled out nickels on Halloween, and though the neighborhood kids thought it was icky how the candy he gave out was unwrapped, nobody dared roll him with toilet paper. He had a reputation as being a good neighbor.

"I used to shovel his driveway in the winter," said one boy. "I'd ring his doorbell and he usually answered the door himself. At first some of our parents did tell us to stay away. You know, they were worried about the gangsters. But I have nothing against him."

Coming to terms with low-flying helicopters swooping down four or five times a day, Club Drive liked having Gambino on the turf. He brought good protection with plenty of police surveillance. As soon as the kids could tell the difference between a wheelman and a Fed—the Feds drove Fords—

nobody worried much about drive-bys. But a mother was a mother, and with the gang war all over the papers, she told her son not to shovel snow at Mr. Gambino's until the heat cooled.

Snow piled up over the course of the Gallo-Colombo war, heaping suffering on Old Man Gambino. If only all five families were as honorable as his, so disciplined that when he waved a hand, people appeared from nowhere to do his bidding.

This kind of incessant feuding would be the death of them all unless steps were taken, streamlining all five families into one with the fat sliced off, leaving a lean organization as it was in the old days under the great bandit chieftain Salvatore Maranzano, who had ruled New York City as *capo di tutti capi*, boss of all bosses, before Lucky Luciano killed him off to create the Commission.

Gambino wanted peace. His heart couldn't take the strain of endless gang war. He placed eleven pills on the table to show the visiting FBI agent, whom he had invited to join him for his morning breakfast of a grapefruit, a toasted English muffin, and coffee. He took another bottle of pills from his pocket, explaining, "I have to take thirty pills a day."

Gambino had to take pills to even walk outside his home. He could not travel or make any plans because he did not know from one day to the next where he would be. He could be in the hospital tomorrow just as well as at his own home. His brother Joey had just suffered a heart attack. His brother Paul was sick too. When the Fed asked Gambino if he would mind any further visits to his home, Gambino said, "I'm always around, I never go anyplace, I'm a sick, sick man." If only he had no heart at all.

Kid Blast never should've cut his hair. Tony Bernardo convinced him it would grow back but never did. The Greek, free
to throw an insult from the safety of Witness Protection said
his hair plugs looked like "dirty rings." Blast stuck it out on
President Street. The rough patches filled in, enough so that
"he looked like that lead in the Scorsese movie where De
Niro's in debt to the bookie," said Detective Bartels.

Surviving the odds in the two years since Joey's death, Blast
was looking good, but now Charlie the Moose was on his ass
as new boss of the Colombo Family, whatever that was worth
anymore, declaring that all "fall in line or fall in the streets."

After fifteen years of gang war, Gallo underboss Mooney
Cutrone decided he had finally had enough of being a Gallo,
of watching *Batman* reruns, playing pinochle, and eating
Umberto's pasta. Going to the mattresses was bad for his aging back. He left President Street for good, taking Sammy the
Syrian with him and twenty-three other Gallos. Blast was
furious after having taken care of the gang, keeping them out
of drugs, and reportedly forking over the greens to compensate for lost rackets.

"We are very honorable," Blast told one NYPD investigator.

"You think you're the Godfather. You shouldn't go to the
movies. You're going to get killed one of these days."

"If that's the way it's got to be, then that's the way it's got
to be."

Kid Blast went to the mattresses, holing up at Roy Roy's
Social Club with the last of the fifteen Gallos, aging Mod

Squaders, hanging on until they were so broke that they had to leech off the hot-dog man who worked on the corner of President Street until the vendor walked over to headquarters and demanded his sixty-dollar tab. By then, the Five Families were so sick of Gallos, they decided to give Blast whatever the hell he wanted.

In his mid-forties, Kid Blast, as the legend goes, was at last made a man, not by the Colombos but Chin Gigante, boss of Greenwich Village. Nicknamed the Oddfather, Chin ran the Genovese Family from Village social clubs, then wandered onto MacDougal Street in his bathrobe while muttering to himself, feigning insanity to keep the Feds off his tail. Crazy Joe would've been proud. Today, Kid Blast lives on, his notorious past dissolved into legend, having stayed out of trouble and out of the press for three decades.

In the city's effort to clean up the stinking Gowanus, a sewer line was dug into Columbia Street in the 1970s. The open trench became a hive of rats and mosquitoes. In time, the entire block of President Street by the waterfront would be razed, as if to eliminate any lingering trace of the Gallos. Then, after the sewer was filled back in, Columbia Street began its twenty-year rise as a choice spot to live for modern-day Brooklyn hipsters. In 2008, the Swedish furniture giant IKEA inched in on Gallo turf, far more successful than Junior's attempted cross-dressing kamikaze raids on the Dormitory.

Sources

Selected Bibliography

AMBURN, ELLIS. *Subterranean Kerouac: The Hidden Life of Jack Kerouac*. New York: St. Martin's Press, 1998.

ARONSON, HARVEY. *The Killing of Joey Gallo*. New York: Putnam, 1973.

BARNES, LEROY "NICKY," and TOM FOLSOM. *Mr. Untouchable*. New York: Rugged Land, 2007.

BARZINI, LUIGI. *From Caesar to the Mafia: Sketches of Italian Life*. New York: Library Press, 1971.

———. *The Italians*. 1st American ed., New York: Atheneum, 1964.

BLUMENTHAL, RALPH. *The Stork Club: America's Most Famous Nightspot and the Lost World of Café Society*. Boston : Little, Brown, 2000.

BONANNO, BILL. *Bound by Honor: A Mafioso's Story*. New York: St. Martin's Press, 1999.

BONANNO, JOSEPH, with SERGIO LALLI. *A Man of Honor: The Autobiography of Joseph Bonanno*. New York: Simon & Schuster, 1983.

BONANNO, ROSALIE, with BEVERLY DONOFRIO. *Mafia Marriage: My Story*. New York: Morrow, 1990.

BRANDT, CHARLES. *"I Heard You Paint Houses": Frank "The Irishman" Sheeran and the Inside Story of the Mafia, the Teamsters, and the Last Ride of Jimmy Hoffa*. Hanover, N.H.: Steerforth Press, 2004.

BRESLIN, JIMMY. *The Gang That Couldn't Shoot Straight*. New York: Viking Press, 1969.

——. *The Good Rat: A True Story*. New York: Ecco, 2008.

BURROUGHS, WILLIAM S., edited by JAMES GRAUER-HOLZ and BARRY MILES. *Naked Lunch, The Restored Text*. 1st ed., New York: Grove Press, 2001.

CANNATO, VINCENT. *The Ungovernable City: John Lindsay and His Struggle to Save New York*. New York: Basic Books, 2001.

CAPECI, JERRY. *The Complete Idiot's Guide to the Mafia*. 2nd ed., Indianapolis, IN: Alpha Books, 2004.

CARO, ROBERT A. *The Power Broker: Robert Moses and the Fall of New York*. New York: Vintage Books, 1974.

CLEAVER, ELDRIDGE. *Soul on Ice*. New York: McGraw-Hill, 1967.

DALEY, ROBERT. *Target Blue: An Insider's View of the N.Y.P.D.* New York: Delacorte Press, 1973.

DEARBORN, MARY. *Mailer: A Biography*. Boston: Houghton Mifflin, 1999.

DELOACH, CARTHA. *Hoover's FBI: The Inside Story by Hoover's Trusted Lieutenant*. Washington, D.C.: Regnery, 1995.

DIAPOULOS, PETER, and STEVEN LINAKIS. *The Sixth Family*. New York: Dutton, 1976.

ELLISON, HARLAN. *Memos from Purgatory: Two Journeys of Our Times*, Evanston, Ill.: Regency Books, 1961.

EVANS, ROBERT. *The Kid Stays in the Picture*. New York: Hyperion, 1994.

GAGE, NICHOLAS. *The Mafia Is Not an Equal Opportunity Employer*. New York: McGraw-Hill, 1971.

GAVIN, JAMES. *Intimate Nights: The Golden Age of New York Cabaret*. New York: Grove Weidenfeld, 1991.

GINSBERG, ALLEN, edited by GORDON BALL. *Journals: early fifties, early sixties*. New York: Grove Press, 1977.

GINSBERG, ALLEN, edited by DAVID CARTER. *Spontaneous Mind: Selected Interviews, 1958-1996*. New York: HarperCollins, 2001.

GITLIN, TODD. *The Sixties: Years of Hope, Days of Rage*. Toronto, New York: Bantam Books, 1987.

GODDARD, DONALD. *Joey*. New York: Harper & Row, 1974.

GORDON, LORRAINE, as told to BARRY SINGER. *Alive at the Village Vanguard: My Life In and Out of Jazz Time*. Milwaukee, Wisc.: Hal Leonard Corp., 2006.

GOTTEHRER, BARRY. *The Mayor's Man*. Garden City, N.Y.: Doubleday, 1975.

GUEVARA, CHE. *Guerrilla Warfare*. Lincoln: University of Nebraska Press, 1998.

HESS, HENNER. *Mafia and Mafiosi: Origin, Power, and Myth*. New York: New York University Press, 1998.

HEYLIN, CLINTON. *Bob Dylan: Behind the Shades Revisited*. New York: William Morrow, 2001.

JOEY, with DAVID FISHER. *Joey the Hitman: The Autobiography of a Mafia Killer*. New York: Thunder's Mouth Press, 2002.

JOHNSON, MALCOLM M. *Crime on the Labor Front*. New York: McGraw-Hill, 1950.

KENNEDY, ROBERT F. *The Enemy Within*. New York: Harper, 1960.

KEROUAC, JACK. *On the Road*. New York: Viking Press, 1957.

———. *The Subterraneans*. New York: Grove Press, 1958.

———, edited by ANN CHARTERS. *Selected Letters, 1940–1956*. New York: Viking, 1995.

KOBLER, JOHN. *Capone: The Life and World of Al Capone*. New York: Putnam, 1971.

LEWIS, NORMAN. *The Honored Society: A Searching Look at the Mafia*. New York: Putnam, 1964.

MAAS, PETER. *Underboss: Sammy the Bull Gravano's Story of Life in the Mafia*. Thorndike, Me: Thorndike Press, 1997.

———. *The Valachi Papers*. New York: Putnam, 1968.

MAILER, NORMAN. *The Time of Our Time*. New York: Random House, 1998.

———. *Advertisements for Myself*. New York: Putnam, 1959.

MARTIN, LINDA, and KERRY SEGRAVE. *Anti-rock: The Opposition to Rock 'n' Roll*. Hamden, Conn.: Archon Books, 1988.

MARTIN, RAYMOND V. *Revolt in the Mafia*. New York: Duell, Sloan and Pearce, 1963.

MESKIL, PAUL S. *The Luparelli Tapes: The True Story of the Mafia Hitman Who Contracted to Kill Both Joey Gallo and His Own Wife*. Chicago: Playboy Press, 1976.

MINGUS, CHARLES, edited by NEL KING. *Beneath the Underdog*. New York: Penguin Books, 1971.

MORGAN, BILL. *The Beat Generation in New York: A Walking Tour of Jack Kerouac's City*. San Francisco: City Lights Books, 1997.

MULLIGAN, GERRY. *Jeru: In the Words of Gerry Mulligan, An Oral Autobiography*. Washington, D.C.: Library of Congress.

PODELL-RABER, MICKEY, with CHARLES PIGNONE. *The Copa: Jules Podell and the Hottest Club North of Havana*. New York: Collins, 2007.

POLSKY, NED. *Hustlers, Beats, and Others*. Chicago: Aldine, 1967.

PUZO, MARIO. *The Godfather*. New York: Putnam, 1969.

RAAB, SELWYN. *Five Families: The Rise, Decline, and Resurgence of America's Most Powerful Mafia Empires*. New York: Thomas Dunne Books, 2005.

REICH, WILHELM. *Listen, Little Man! A Document from the Archives of the Orgone Institute*. New York: Orgone Institute Press, 1948.

REPPETTO, THOMAS. *American Mafia: A History of Its Rise to Power*. New York: H. Holt, 2004.

ROBBINS, MICHAEL W., editor. *Brooklyn: A State of Mind*. New York: Workman, 2001.

SALERNO, RALPH, and JOHN S. TOMPKINS. *The Crime Confederation: Cosa Nostra and Allied Operations in Organized Crime*. Garden City, N.Y.: Doubleday, 1969.

SANTORO, GENE. *Myself When I Am Real: The Life and Music of Charles Mingus*. New York: Oxford University Press, 2000.

SAYRE, NORA. *Sixties Going on Seventies*. New York: Arbor House, 1973.

SCHLESINGER, ARTHUR M., JR. *Robert Kennedy and His Times*, Boston: Houghton Mifflin, 1978.

SCORZA, S. E., compiler. *Mafia: The Government's Secret File on Organized Crime.* New York: Collins, 2007.

SEEDMAN, ALBERT A., and PETER HELLMAN. *Chief!* New York: Fields Books, 1974.

SHORT, BOBBY, with ROBERT MACKINTOSH. *Bobby Short, The Life and Times of a Saloon Singer.* New York: C. Potter, 1995.

STEINBERG, DAVID. *The Book of David.* New York: Simon & Schuster, 2007.

SUKENICK, RONALD. *Down and In: Life in the Underground.* New York: Beech Tree Books, 1987.

SUTTON, WILLIE, with EDWARD LINN. *Where the Money Was.* New York: Viking Press, 1976.

TALESE, GAY. *Honor Thy Father.* New York: World, 1971.

THOMAS, EVAN. *Robert Kennedy: His Life.* New York: Simon & Schuster, 2000.

TOSCHES, NICK. *Dino: Living High in the Dirty Business of Dreams.* New York: Doubleday, 1992.

TURKUS, BURTON B., and SID FEDER. *Murder, Inc., The Story of "The Syndicate."* New York: Farrar, Straus & Young, 1951.

WAKEFIELD, DAN. *New York in the Fifties.* Boston: Houghton Mifflin/Seymour Lawrence, 1992.

WARHOL, ANDY, and PAT HACKETT. *POPism: The Warhol Sixties.* Orlando: Harcourt, 1980.

WELCH, NEIL, and DAVID MARSTON. *Inside Hoover's FBI: The Top Field Chief Reports.* Garden City, N.Y.: Doubleday, 1984.

Selected Articles

ADLER, RENATA. "The Screen: Norman Mailer's Mailer: 'Wild 90,' Another Ad for Writer, Bows." *New York Times*, 8 January 1968.

Advertisement, "Russian Tea Room." *Evergreen Review*, volume 5, no. 16, January-February 1961.

Advertisement, "Fair Play for Cuba Committee." *Evergreen Review*, volume 4, no. 15, November-December 1960.

ALDEN, ROBERT. " 'Village' Tension Upsets Residents." *New York Times*, 29 September 1959.

ALLAN, JOHN H. "Profits of 'The Godfather'; $1-Million a Day Pours into Box Offices." *New York Times*, 16 April 1972.

ANDERSON, DAVID. "35 Bookies Seized in Sunrise Raids." *New York Times*, 28 October 1964.

ARNOLD, MARTIN. "Auburn Prisoners Hold 50 Hostages Eight Hours." *New York Times*, 5 November 1970.

————. "Gallos' Quarters Open But Empty." *New York Times*, 11 December 1963.

"At Home with Marta and Jerry Orbach." *New York Post*, 7 June 1969.

ATKINSON, BROOKS. "Theatre: The Jungles of the City." *New York Times*, 27 September 1957.

"Auburn Is Quiet After Outbreak." *New York Times*, 6 November 1970.

BERGER, MEYER. "Anastasia Slain in a Hotel Here; Led Murder, Inc." *New York Times*, 26 October 1957.

BLUMENFELD, RALPH. "The Gallo Gang Finds Tough Men at the Top." *New York Post*, 6 October 1961.

————. "His New Life Style Died Young." *New York Post*, 8 April 1972.

————. "Gallo Relatives Grieve at Bier." *New York Times*, 10 April 1972.

BONFANTE, JORDAN. "Alright Already, The Mob Is Heroes." *Life*, 9 February 1962.

"Boy, 16, Arraigned as Gang Slayer." *New York Times*, 14 May 1950.

BRANDT, CHARLES. "Who Killed Joey Gallo?" *Playboy*, 1 August 2005.

BREASTED, MARY. "Gallo Factions Declare a Truce After Series of Shootings in Which One Was Killed and Seven Were Wounded." *New York Times*, 10 November 1974.

BRESLIN, JIMMY. "The Real Mafia Sells Heroin, Not Books." *Newsday*, 18 August 1972.

"Brooklyn Mafia Chief Joseph Colombo." *New York Times*, 25 March 1970.

BUCKLEY, THOMAS. "Ex-Detective Chief Says Gang War Dooms Gallos." *New York Times*, 15 August 1963.

———. "2 in Brooklyn Gangs Slain as War Grows." *New York Times*, 10 August 1963.

CHRISTESON, WAYNE. "Married to the Mob." *Nashville Scene*, 3 May 2007.

CIOFFI, EDWARD, and LYNN LEONARD. "Searching for Tony." *New York Mirror*, 14 April 1962.

CLARK, ALFRED. "6 Men Arraigned in Tavern Attack." *New York Times*, 22 August 1961.

———. "2 Held on $100,000 in Police Assault." *New York Times*, 24 August 1961

———. "Gallo Sentencing Delayed by Court." *New York Times*, 20 August 1963.

———. "Brooklyn Patrolman Wounded as Three Flee Barroom Fight." *New York Times*, 21 August 1961.

COOK, FRED J. "A Family Business: Hijacking, Bookmaking, Policy, Dice Games, Loan-Sharking and Special Contracts." *New York Times*, 4 June 1972.

———. "Larry Gallo, Crazy Joe and Kid Blast: Robin Hoods or Real Tough Boys?" *New York Times Magazine*, 23 October 1966.

———. "They Got Joe!—Is the War On?" *New York Times*, 4 July 1971.

COUTROS, PETER. "Keening and Tears for a Still-Dapper Gallo." *New York Daily News*, 10 April 1972.

"Crazy Like a Clam." *Time*. 24 November 1961.

CURTIS, CHARLOTTE. "The Last Delicious Days of Joey Gallo." *Harper's Bazaar*, 1971.

"Death Throes of the Gallo Mob." *Life*, 30 August 1963.

"Deportation Quiz on Over Gallo Protest." *New York Daily News*, 30 September 1961.

DOTY, ROBERT. "Gunman Is Sought as Gallo Witness." *New York Times*, 12 December 1963.

————. "16 in Gallo Gang Seized to Halt War on Profacis." *New York Times*, 11 December 1963.

DUNCAN, VAL. "Larry Gallo Quits Jail; Rearrested on the Spot." *Newsday*, 2 December 1963.

DUREY, ALLEN. "Juke Box Dealer Says Hoodlums Beat Him to Gain a Partnership." *New York Times*, 18 February 1959.

"Eboli Is 15th Gangland Victim in a Year." *New York Times*, 17 July 1972.

EGAN, CY, et al. "Murder by Mistake." *New York Post*, 15 August 1972.

EKLIND, DAVID. "Wilhelm Reich—The Psychoanalyst as Revolutionary." *New York Times*, 18 April 1971.

ELLISON, HARLAN. "My Day in Stir, or Buried in the Tombs." *Village Voice*, 29 September 1960.

"Excerpts from Testimony Given Yesterday at the Crime Commission Hearing." *New York Times*, 19 December 1952.

"Ex-Convict Seized in Policy Ring Raid." *New York Times*, 26 March 1952.

FARRELL, WILLIAM. "Colombo Shot, Gunman Slain at Columbus Circle Rally Site." *New York Times*, 29 June 1971.

————. "Police Say Johnson Took Pictures of Colombo Before Shooting." *New York Times*, 1 July 1971.

FASO, FRANK, and PAUL MESKIL. "Cops & Mob Wait & Wonder: Who's Next?" *New York Daily News*, 30 June 1971.

————. "Gallo Put Victims in 3-Wring Circus, Starring Lion." *New York Daily News*, April 1972.

FEDERICI, WILLIAM. "2 More Gang Rubouts as Gallo, 2 Are Buried." *New York Daily News*, 11 April 1972.

FERRETTI, FRED. "Colombo's Son Condemns Police View of Shooting." *New York Times*, 21 July 1971.

————. "Italian Group Got Gallo Aid for Day." *New York Times*, 9 April 1972.

————. "Rally Day Crowd Reacts with Sorrow and Anger." *New York Times*, 29 June 1971.

"5 Shots from Truck Hurt Ex-Convicts." *New York Times*, 20 May 1963.

FLATLEY, GUY. "Making a Racket Over Hackett." *New York Times*, 12 March 1972.

FLEMING, THOMAS J. Case of the Debatable Brooklyn D.A. *New York Times*, 19 March 1967.

"Flight to Harlem." *Time*, 3 October 1960.

FOSBURGH, LACEY. "Gang Figure Goes on Witness Stand." *New York Times*, 27 September 1972.

———. "Killer of Gallo Identified as 4 Are Indicted After Inquiry on Slaying." *New York Times*, 14 December 1972.

———. "Mrs. Gallo Heard in Trial of Aide." *New York Times*, 13 September 1972.

———. "Trial of 'Friend' of Gallo Begins." *New York Times*, 7 September 1972.

———. "Witness Relates How Colombo Gang Slew Gallo." *New York Times*, 26 September 1972.

FREEMAN, IRA HENRY. "Brothers Anastasia—Toughest of the Toughs." *New York Times*, 14 December 1952.

GAGE, NICHOLAS. "Colombo 'Family' Seeking Peace in Classic Style—By More Killing." *New York Times*, 7 November 1976.

———. "Colombo Gunplay Is Linked to Revenge." *New York Times*, 6 June 1972.

———. "Colombo's Refusal to Buy Off Gallo for $100,000 Cited." *New York Times*, 5 July 1971.

———. "Five in Gallo Gang Named on Death List." *New York Times*, 26 April 1972.

———. "Five Mafia Families Open Rosters to New Members." *New York Times*, 21 March 1976.

———. "Four Men and a Woman Arrested at Alleged Hide-Out of Colombo Family." *New York Times*, 25 April 1972.

———. "Gallo-Colombo Feud Said to Have Been Renewed." *New York Times*, 29 June 1971.

———. "Gambino Believed Seeking Single Mafia Family Here." *New York Times*, 8 December 1972.

———. "Gambino: Quiet Man in Spotlight." *New York Times*, 25 July 1971.

———. "Gang War Could Be a Rough One; Gallo-Colombo Fight Would Draw on '60's Experience." *New York Times*, 12 April 1972.

———. "Grudges Against Gallo Date to 'War' with Profaci." *New York Times*, 8 April 1972.

———. "Guard of Colombo Quoted as Naming Gallo Brothers." *New York Times*, 30 July 1971.

———. "The Hoods Seem to Be Quarreling; The Shooting Gallery—Six Casualties of the Gangland War." *New York Times*, 16 April 1972.

———. "Key Mafia Figure Tells of 'Wars' and Gallo-Colombo Peace Talks." *New York Times*, 7 July 1975.

———. "Many of Mafiosi Resent Colombo." *New York Times*, 3 July 1971.

———. "Meeting of Colombo Aides Linked to Narcotics Trade." *New York Times*, 16 August 1972.

———. "Police Say Evidence Backs Informant's Gallo Story." 6 May 1972.

———. "Slain Brooklyn Man Described as Colombo 'Family' Associate." *New York Times*, 11 April 1972.

———. "Story of Joe Gallo's Murder." *New York Times*, 3 May 1972.

———. "They Don't Just Kill Each Other; Gang War." *New York Times*, 20 August 1972.

———. "Two Are Hunted in Gallo Murder." *New York Times*, 14 April, 1972.

"Gallo Aide Cited on Pistol Charge." *New York Times*, 26 May 1972.

"Gallo Foe Yields in Gang War Case." *New York Times*, 14 December 1963.

"Gallo Reprisal Held Motive in Shootings." *New York Times*, 3 July 1974.

"Gallo: This Time, the Gang Shot Straight." *New York Times*, 9 April 1972.

"Gang-Style Death Is Reported Here." *New York Times*, 3 May 1972.

GESSNER, PETER. "Espresso Underground Lays Down Party Line." *Village Voice*, 6 July 1961.

"Goings on About Town." *The New Yorker*, August 1960–March 1961.

GRILLO, JEAN BERGANTINI. "Life with Godfather: Carlo Gambino and His Neighbors." *New York Times*, 15 August 1976.

GROVE, GENE. "I Pulled Out a Mezuzah." *Village Voice*, 20 April 1972.

———. "Joey Gallo Goes to Washington." *New York Post*, 10 November 1961.

———. "A Visit with Joey Gallo." *New York Post*, 9 November 1961.

GRUTZNER, CHARLES. "Lunchtime Favorite of Judges Raided; Lacks Wine Permit." *New York Times*, 23 December 1964.

———. "Mafia Is Giving Up Heroin Monopoly." *New York Times*, 2 September 1967.

HALEY, PETER. "Up, Not Over, the Hill: Old-Time Italian Specialty Comes to Court Street." *Brooklyn Phoenix*, 17 November 1977.

HAMILL, PETE. "Bright Lives, Big City." *New York Times*, 2 January 2005.

———. "Brooklyn's Joe Gallo—Young Hoodlum of the Old School." *New York Post*, 27 August 1961.

———. "Goodbye to Joey the Blond." *New York Post*, 10 April 1972.

———. "The Long Goodbye." *New York Post*, 11 April 1972.

HART, HOWARD. "Camus: The Right Side of Our Face Has Fallen Off." *Village Voice*, 13 January 1960.

HELLMAN, PETER. "It Is Very Hard to Smile at Albert Seedman When He Is Not Smiling at You." *New York Times Magazine*, 30 April 1972.

HENDRICKS, ALFRED. "Police Say Four Saw Gallo Mobster Slain." *New York Post*, 5 October 1961.

———. "Gallo Gang to Grand Jury." *New York Post*, 11 October 1961.

HENTOFF, NAT. "Lenny Bruce and the Aging Hipsters." *Village Voice*, 6 April 1960.

HOFMANN, PAUL. "Folk Singers Riot in Washington Sq." *New York Times*, 10 April 1961.

———. "Opinions Differ on Gallo's Role." *New York Times*, 13 August 1966.

"How a Wheelman Turned Canary." *New York Times*, 7 May 1972.

"Hundreds Risk Jail in Civil Defense Protest." *Village Voice*, 11 May 1960.

IVINS, MOLLY. "Red Hook Survives Hard Times into New Era." *New York Times*, 16 November 1981.

JOHNSON, THOMAS A. "Two Gallos Acted as Peacemakers; Brothers Enlisted to Calm Youths in East New York." *New York Times*, 6 August 1966.

KANTER, NATHAN. "Hood Tony Bender Missing Since Sunday, Wife Reports."

KATZ, LEONARD, and JOHN MULLANE. "Muted Farewell for Joe Gallo." *New York Post*, 10 April 1977.

KAUFMAN, MICHAEL: "Profaci's Roots Deep in Brooklyn." *New York Times*, 18 August 1964.

———. "Troubles Persist in Prison at Auburn." *New York Times*, 17 May 1971.

KIERNAN, JOSEPH, and SIDNEY KLINE. "Gallo Loud in Hall, Silent to Jury." *New York Daily News*, 12 October 1961.

———. "Heat on Gallos, Cowering without Heaters." *New York Post*, 6 October 1961.

———. "Raid Gallo Ratholes, Grab 13." *New York Daily News*, 11 October 1961.

KIERNAN, JOSEPH, and WILLIAM FEDERICI. "Immigration Rap Jails Pa Gallo." *New York Daily News*, 13 September 1961.

KIFNER, JOHN. "Lindsay Defends Gallo Peace Role." *New York Times*, 27 August 1966.

KIRK, DON. "Tony Bender Knew His Number Was Up." *New York Post*, 15 April 1962.

———. "Gang Victim Is Dead in Jersey Shooting." *New York Times*, 27 July 1963.

———. "Koota Is Rebuffed by Gallo Brothers." *New York Times*, 18 August 1966.

KIRKMAN, EDWARD. "Gallos and Colombos Vow Duel to the Death." *New York Daily News*, 16 August 1972.

———. "Mob Killed Two by Mistake." *New York Daily News*, 15 August 1972.

———. "Mob War Now Perils Public." *New York Daily News*, 15 August 1972.

KREBS, ALBIN. "Brooklyn Sniper Kills Negro Boy in Race Disorder." *New York Times*, 22 July 1966.

———. "Notes on People." *New York Times*, 18 March 1972.

"Larry Gallo Dies in Sleep at 41." *New York Times*, 19 May 1968.

LEHMANN-HAUPT, CHRISTOPHER. "Back into the Old Orgone Box." *New York Times*, 4 January 1971.

LICHTENSTEIN, GRACE. "Shooting Blends Fact with Fiction in Little Italy." *New York Times*, 8 April 1972.

LIFF, BOB, and JAMYE WOLFSON. "New York Chess in Concrete." *Newsday*, 4 December 1988.

LUTZ, H. B. "The Man Is Mad!" *Village Voice*, 28 October 1959.

KOLTNOW, BARRY. "For Rickles, Insult Is Far from Injury." *The Orange County Register*, 6 September 1990.

McCAFFREY, JAMES. "Gallo, at Court, Denies Gang War." *New York Times*, 12 October 1961.

———. "Gallo Witnesses Heard by Inquiry." *New York Times*, 14 October 1961.

MAILER, NORMAN. "An Open Letter to JFK and Castro." *Village Voice*, 27 April 1961.

———. "The White Negro." *Dissent*, spring 1957.

"Man Held in Dockworker Slaying." *New York Times*, 18 March 1951.

MESKIL, PAUL. "A Mobster Talks: Colombo Shot, The War Is On." *New York Daily News*, 25 November 1974.

———. "A Mobster Talks: 'They're Out to Kill Me . . .'" *New York Daily News*, 24 November 1974.

MONTGOMERY, PAUL. "1,000 Policemen Move in to Stem Brooklyn Unrest." *New York Times*, 23 July 1966.

MONTGOMERY, PAUL. "Italians to Hold Rally Tomorrow." *New York Times*, 28 June 1970.

———. "Italian-Americans Ready for Colorful Unity Day." *New York Times*, 29 June 1970.

———. "Thousands of Italians Here Rally Against Ethnic Slurs." *New York Times*, 30 June 1970.

MORRISON, CHESTER. "The Case of Brooklyn's Thrill Killers." *Look*.

NAVASKY, VICTOR. "The Politics of Justice." *New York Times*, 5 May 1974.

NEUGEBAUER, WILLIAM, and JACK SMEE. "2 Gun Down Cop, Flee Muscle Job." *New York Daily News*, 21 August 1961.

NICHOLS, MARY. "City of Life or City of Death?" *Village Voice*, 28 December 1961.

———. "Is Modern Man Meaningless? Village Forum Packs Church." *Village Voice*, 30 December 1959.

"Norman Mailer Is Found Sane; Author Bailed in Wife Stabbing." *New York Times*, 10 December 1960.

OELSNER, LESLIE. "'Facts' About Colombo's Attacker Vary." *New York Times*, 29 June 1971.

"Our Friend Joey Gallo." *Time*, 17 April 1972.

PACE, ERIC. "Albert Gallo, the 'Kid Brother,' Picks Up Mantle for 'Honor' of Mafia Family." *New York Times*, 17 August 1972.

———. "Gambling Figure Found Slain; City's Gang-Style Murders Rise to 8." *New York Times*, 20 April 1972.

———. "Joe Gallo Is Shot to Death in Little Italy Restaurant." *New York Times*, 8 April 1972.

———. "3 More Gangland Killings Bring Total to 6 in 5 Days." *New York Times*, 11 April 1972.

———. "The Men Who Fight Mafiosi and Killers." *New York Times*, 16 August 1972.

PEARSON, DREW. "Mobsters Meeting in Miami." *Washington Post*, 2 February 1962.

———. "Surrenders in Slaying." *New York Times*, 17 March 1951.

———. "Brooklyn Slayer Pleads Guilty." *New York Times*, 8 August 1951.

PELLECK, CARL, and TOM TOPOR. "Joe Gallo Slain." *New York Post*, 7 April 1972.

PELLECK, CARL, et al. "Guard Actor and Wife in the Gallo Slaying." *New York Post*, 12 April 1972.

PERLMUTTER, EMANUEL. "A Key Gang Figure Slain in Brooklyn," 17 July 1972.

———. "Murder Witness Says Gallo's Guard Was Armed." *New York Times*, 14 September 1972.

———. "Police Say a Hired Killer Slew 2 in Error." *New York Times*, 15 August 1972.

———. "Roots of the Gallo-Profaci War: Youth vs. Age, Need vs. Plenty." 11 December 1963.

———. "Run Gangsters Out of City, Angry Mayor Tells Police." *New York Times*, 17 August 1972.

PILEGGI, NICHOLAS. "The Making of 'The Godfather'—Sort of a Home Movie." *New York Times*, 15 August 1971.

"Pistol Is Clue in Slaying of Policy Banker." *New York Post*, 5 November 1959.

"Police Break Up Harlem Crowd as Groups Mingle." *New York Times*, 22 September 1960.

"Police Raid Gallos, Arrest 14 in Gang." *New York Times*, 16 November 1961.

"Profaci Dies of Cancer; Led Feuding Brooklyn Mob." *New York Times*, 8 June 1962.

QUINN, SALLY. "Journalism's New Nation." *Washington Post*, 26 April 1972.

"Release Jukebox Boys; Cops Just Needling 'Em." *New York Daily News*, 14 April 1959.

ROBINSON, DOUGLAS. "Mafia Believed Behind the Italian-American Protests Over 'Harassment.'" *New York Times*, 19 July 1970.

ROSS, EDWIN, and JOSEPH KIERNAN. "Gallo Stooge Tried to Kill Boss and His Number's Up." *New York Daily News*, 24 August 1961.

ROTH, JACK. "Norman Mailer Sent to Bellevue Over His Protest in Wife Knifing." *New York Times*, 23 November 1960.

SCADUTO, ANTHONY. "The Gangsters' Battle of Brooklyn." *New York Post*, 18 October 1961.

SCHUMACH, MURRAY. "Lindsay Walk in Brooklyn Stirs Pros and Cons." *New York Times*, 19 August 1966.

SHEAHAN, DENIS. "The Gang Shot Straight to Get Gallo." *Women's Wear Daily*, 10 April 1972.

SINGER, HARRY. "Scimone Gives Up in Attack on Gallo." *New York Daily Mirror*, 7 October 1961.

"$65,000,000 Roads Proposed by Moses for City's Defense." *New York Times*, 11 November 1940.

SLATER, SIDNEY, with QUENTIN REYNOLDS. "My Life Inside the Mob." *Saturday Evening Post*, 24-31 August 1963.

STEPHENS, M. G. "Conrad's List." *Boston Review*, December 2003/January 2004.

"Suit by Gallo Charges 'Unusual Punishment'." *New York Times*, 29 August 1964.

TALLMER, JERRY. "There Is No Godfather." *New York Post*, 8 April 1972.

"13 in Gallo Gang Arrested in Raid." *New York Times*, 11 October 1961.

"13 in Gallo Gang Ask Lower Bail." *New York Times*, 18 October 1961.

TOPOR, TOM. "New York's Mob Wars." *New York Post*, 18 April 1972.

"$25,000,000 Artery Begun in Brooklyn." *New York Times*, 21 August 1946.

"Two Are Indicted in Gallo Attack." *New York Times*, 6 October 1961.

VAN GELDER, LAWRENCE. "Prison Has History of Riot and Reform." *New York Times*, 5 November 1970.

———. "Colombo: A Man with Several Roles." *New York Times*, 29 June 1971.

WEILER, A. H. "The Orbachs' Pal Joey." *New York Times*, 19 March 1972.

WHITNEY, CRAIG. "Italians Picket F.B.I. Office Here." *New York Times*, 2 May 1970.

WILSON, EARL. "Last Chat with a Mobster." *New York Post,* 7 April 1972.

WISE, DAVID. "Says Juke-Box Goons Beat Him So Long They Took Coffee Break." *New York Herald Tribune,* 18 February 1959.

ZINGG, DAVID. "A Teen-Age Gang from the Inside." *Look,* 23 August 1955.

ZION, SIDNEY E. "Police Scoff at Idea Persico Could Be 'Conned'." *New York Times,* 5 August 1965.

Selected Films, Sound Recordings, Television, and Websites

Baker, Fred. *Lenny Bruce: Without Tears.* New York: First Run Features, 1972.

Bruce, Lenny. *Live at the Curran Theater.* Berkeley, Calif.: Fantasy Records, 1971

The Daily Show. Comedy Central. New York: 31 May 2007.

Hathaway, Henry. *Kiss of Death.* Twentieth-Century Fox, 1947.

Pennebaker, D. A. "Norman Mailer: At First Light." Pennebaker/Hegedus Films. http://phfilms.blogspot.com/2008/05/norman-mailer-at-first-light.html (1 Feb 2008).

Selected Government Archives, Trial Transcripts and Files

People of the State of New York v. Joseph Gallo, Sidney Slater, Michael Albergo and Ali Waffa. Court of General Sessions, New York County, N.Y.

People v. Michael Albergo, Ali Waffa, Hyman Powell. Court of General Sessions, New York County, N.Y.

People of the State of New York v. Joseph Gallo. City Magistrate's Court of New York, Borough of Brooklyn, Flatbush Part.

United States. Congress. Senate. Committee on Government Operations. Permanent Subcommittee on Investigations. Organized Crime and Illicit Traffic in Narcotics. *Hearings before the Permanent Subcommittee on Investigations of the Committee on*

Government Operations, United States Senate, Eighty-eighth Congress. U.S. Govt. Print. Off., 1963–1965.

United States. Congress. Senate. Select Committee on Improper Activities in the Labor or Management Field. Investigation of Improper Activities in the Labor or Management Field: *Hearings Before the Select Committee on Improper Activities in the Labor or Management Field, Eighty-Fifth-Congress.* Washington, D.C.: U.S. Govt. Print. Off., 1957–1960.

U.S. Department of Justice, Federal Bureau of Investigation, Washington, D.C. File No. 92-1610: Joseph Gregory Gallo.

U.S. Department of Justice, Federal Bureau of Investigation, Washington, D.C. File No. 92-3405: Carlo Gambino.

U.S. Department of Justice, Federal Bureau of Investigation, Washington, D.C. File No. 92-2834: Joseph Profaci.

United States of America v. Carmine J. Persico, Jr., et al., Defendants. United States District Court for the Eastern District of New York.

Acknowledgments

My deepest gratitude goes to those who served in the NYPD, Albert Seedman and Charles Bartels, and in the FBI, Bernard Welsh. Thank you all for bringing me back to the mean streets. I'm indebted to Nicholas Gage, who shed light on his coverage on the Gallos for the *New York Times* over coffee at a Greek diner. Thanks to Dennis Dillon, Sterling Johnson, and Henner Hess, and to Jim Miller at the New School for insight into the madness of the sixties.

I'm grateful to Ken Cobb and Michael Lorenzini at the Municipal Archives, a stop on my journey into the naked city's lowlife. For the highlife, thanks to the staff at the Billy Rose Theatre Collection at the New York Public Library for the Performing Arts, also to Thomas Angelo at the Brooklyn Public Library. Thanks to Brendan, Justin, Niko, Mirella, and Mark Seliger, who took my mug shot, and Brian Chojnowski, who came up with a cover worthy of the beats.

It's a privilege to work with the dedicated creative team at Weinstein Books, who saw the big picture from the beginning. Thanks to Judy Hottensen, Kristin Powers, Katie Finch,

Danielle Plafsky, and Adrian Palacios. To Richard Florest, who saw Joey and his brothers as characters in a Godard film, thanks for your fine eye. Thanks especially to Harvey and Bob Weinstein.

To my agent, Zoë Pagnamenta, I owe the pleasure of working with the best.

To the Folsom Family, I couldn't have done it without you.

Thanks to Lily, mad to love.